First World War
and Army of Occupation
War Diary
France, Belgium and Germany

49 DIVISION
Divisional Troops
247 Brigade Royal Field Artillery
1 May 1915 - 30 June 1916

WO95/2782/1

The Naval & Military Press Ltd
www.nmarchive.com
Published in association with The National Archives

Published by

The Naval & Military Press Ltd

Unit 10 Ridgewood Industrial Park,

Uckfield, East Sussex,

TN22 5QE England

Tel: +44 (0) 1825 749494

www.naval-military-press.com

www.nmarchive.com

This diary has been reprinted in facsimile from the original. Any imperfections are inevitably reproduced and the quality may fall short of modern type and cartographic standards.

© **Crown Copyright**
Images reproduced by permission of The National Archives, London, England, 2015.

Contents

Document type	Place/Title	Date From	Date To
Heading	49th Division 3rd W.R. Field Arty Bde Vol 1 1-31.5.15		
War Diary	Fleurbaix	01/05/1915	31/05/1915
Miscellaneous	49th Division 1/3rd W.R. Bde R.F.A. Vol II 1-30.6.15		
War Diary	Fleurbaix	01/06/1915	29/06/1915
War Diary	Caestre	30/06/1915	30/06/1915
Heading	49th Division 3rd W.R. Bde R.F.A. Vol III 1-31-7-15		
War Diary	Watou	01/07/1915	08/07/1915
War Diary	Elverdinghe	08/07/1915	31/07/1915
Heading	49th Division 1/3rd W.R. Bde R.F.A. Vol IV August 15		
Miscellaneous	War Diary for August 1915		
War Diary	Elverdinghe	01/08/1915	31/08/1915
Operation(al) Order(s)	Operation Orders by Lieut. Colonel Charles Clifford. W.R. R.F.A. (T) Commanding Left Group.	25/08/1915	25/08/1915
Heading	49th Division 1/3rd W.R. Bde R.F.A. Vol V Sept. 15 V		
Miscellaneous	War Diary 1/3rd West Rid. Bde. R.F.A. 49th (W.R) Division. Septr 1915		
War Diary	Elverdinghe	01/09/1915	30/09/1915
Heading	49th Division 1/3 W.R. Bde R.F.A. Vol VI Oct 15		
Heading	War Diary October 1915 1/3rd West Riding Brigade R.F.A.T.		
War Diary	Elverdinghe	01/10/1915	31/10/1915
Heading	1 Corps. 49th Div. Headquarters. 247th Brigade, R.F.A. July 1916		
War Diary	Englebelmer	01/07/1916	04/07/1916
War Diary	Englebelmer	04/07/1916	05/07/1916
War Diary	Englebelmer	04/07/1916	11/07/1916
War Diary	Mesnil	12/07/1916	31/07/1916
Heading	49th Divisional Artillery. 247th (W.R.) Brigade Royal Field Artillery. August 1916		
War Diary	Mesnil	01/08/1916	08/08/1916
War Diary	Varennes	09/08/1916	27/08/1916
War Diary	Q.22.c 10.20 (Sheet 57d. SE) 1/20000	28/09/1916	28/09/1916
War Diary	Q22 C 1020 (France 57D SE 1/20000)	29/08/1916	31/08/1916
Heading	49th Division 3rd W.R. Bde R.F.A W. Rising Bde. R.F.A. War Diary for November 1915 Vol VII		
War Diary	Elverdinghe	01/11/1915	30/11/1915
Miscellaneous	C.R.A.	15/11/1915	15/11/1915
Miscellaneous	Officer Commanding, 3rd W.R.F.A. Bde.	15/11/1915	15/11/1915
Miscellaneous	Reference Boesinghe 1/10,000 Trench Map.		
Heading	1/3rd West. Rid. Bde R.F.A.T War Diary-December 1915 Vol VIII 49th (N.R) Division.		
Miscellaneous	Dec. 1915, Pl Missing.		
War Diary	Elverdinghe	07/12/1915	01/01/1916
Heading	247th (WR) Bde RFA 1/3rd West Riding Bde R.F.A. War Diary-January 1916 Vol IX 49th (N.R) Division.		
War Diary	Oosthoek	01/01/1916	01/01/1916
War Diary	Rubrouck	02/01/1916	31/01/1916
Heading	1/3rd West Rid Bde R.F.A. War Diary. February 1916 Vol X 49th (W.R) Division.		

Heading	War Diary of 247th (WR) Brigade RFA For February 1916 Vol 22		
War Diary	Rubrouck	01/02/1916	04/02/1916
War Diary	Hangeste Sur Somme	05/02/1916	12/02/1916
War Diary	Hangeste	13/02/1916	15/02/1916
War Diary	Harpon-Ville	16/02/1916	29/02/1916
Heading	1/3rd West Rid Bde. R.F.A. War Diary-March 1916 Vol XI 49th (N.R.) Division.		
War Diary	Harponville	01/03/1916	06/03/1916
War Diary	Molliens Au Bois	07/03/1916	29/03/1916
War Diary	Ipernois	30/03/1916	30/03/1916
War Diary	Pernois	31/03/1916	31/03/1916
Heading	3rd W.R. Bde R.F.A. War Diary-April 1916 Vol XII 49th (N.R) Division.		
War Diary	Pernois	01/04/1916	01/04/1916
War Diary	Berteaucourt	02/04/1916	30/04/1916
Miscellaneous	May/June Missing		
Heading	49th. Divisional Artillery 247th. Brigade R.F.A. September 1916		
Heading	247th (W.R) Bde RFA War Diary-Septr 1916 Vol 17 49th Div.		
War Diary	Q22 C1020. (France 57d SE 1/20000)	01/09/1916	06/09/1916
War Diary	Varennes	07/09/1916	21/09/1916
War Diary	Mesnil	22/09/1916	22/09/1916
War Diary	228a. 9.3 57d SE 1/20000	23/09/1916	30/09/1916
Heading	247th (W.R) Bde RFA. War Diary-October 1916 Vol 18 49th Div.		
War Diary	Q28b93. 57d SE 1/20000	01/10/1916	02/10/1916
War Diary	Varennes Lens 1/10000 Sheet II	03/10/1916	03/10/1916
War Diary	Grouches Lens. 1/100000 Sheet II	03/10/1916	04/10/1916
War Diary	Bavincourt	05/10/1916	05/10/1916
War Diary	France 57d NE 1/20,000	06/10/1916	06/10/1916
War Diary	Bienvillers (France 57d NE 1/20000)	06/10/1916	10/10/1916
War Diary	Gouy-In Artois (Lens Sheet II 1/100,000)	11/10/1916	18/10/1916
War Diary	Bus-En-Artois (Lens Sheet II 1/10000)	18/10/1916	20/10/1916
War Diary	Courcelles (Lens Sheet II 1/100000)	20/10/1916	31/10/1916
Heading	247th (W.R) Bn R.F.A. War Diary November 1916 Vol 19 49th (W.R) Division.		
War Diary	Courcelles (Lens Sheet II 1/100000)	01/11/1916	12/11/1916
War Diary	K 25b 53 (Hebuterne 1/10000)	13/11/1916	19/11/1916
War Diary	Courcelles (Lens II 1/100000)	19/11/1916	22/11/1916
War Diary	Bus-En-Artois	23/11/1916	23/11/1916
War Diary	Humber-Camp	24/11/1916	26/11/1916
War Diary	Bienvillers	27/11/1916	27/11/1916
War Diary	Bienvillers Ref. Map 57d N.E.	27/11/1916	30/11/1916
Miscellaneous	Staff Captain R.A. 49th (W.R.) Division.	02/11/1916	02/11/1916
Heading	War Diary of 247th (WR) Brigade R.F.A. For December 1916 Vol 20		
Heading	247th (WR) Bde RFA. War Diary Decr. 1916 49th Div.		
War Diary	Bienvillers-Au-Bois	01/12/1916	18/12/1916
War Diary	Bienvillers	18/12/1916	21/12/1916
War Diary	Grouches (Lens II 1/100,000)	21/12/1916	31/12/1916
Miscellaneous	O.C. A/247 Battery.	10/12/1916	10/12/1916
Operation(al) Order(s)	49th Divisional Artillery Order No. 45.	09/12/1916	09/12/1916
Miscellaneous	O.C. A/247 Battery.	09/12/1916	09/12/1916
Miscellaneous	D/247 Battery R.F.A.		

Heading	247th (WR) R.F.A. Bde War Diary-January 1917 Vol 21		
War Diary	Grouches (Lens II 1/100000)	01/01/1917	03/01/1917
War Diary	Grouches (Lens II 1/100000) and (France Sheet 51c 1/40,000)	03/01/1917	04/01/1917
War Diary	Grouches Lens II 1/100000	04/01/1917	31/01/1917
War Diary	Grouches	01/02/1917	28/02/1917
Heading	49th Division 247th Brigade R.F.A. May 1915-Feb 1917 Bde Broken Up		
Heading	247th (WR) Bde RFA late 1/3 WR Bde War Diary-May 1916 Vol 13 49th (W.R) Division.		
War Diary	Berteaucourt	01/05/1916	31/05/1916
Heading	49th Divisional Artillery. 247th Brigade. Royal Field Artillery. June 1916		
War Diary	Engelbelmer	01/06/1916	30/06/1916
Miscellaneous	O.C. A.C.V.D. Infty.	27/06/1916	27/06/1916
Miscellaneous	O.C. D/247.	26/06/1916	26/06/1916
Miscellaneous	Programme of Counter Battery Work		
Miscellaneous	Middle Battn. Counter Battery Order for "W" Day	24/06/1916	24/06/1916
Miscellaneous	Programme Counter Battery Order for 'W' Day	26/06/1916	26/06/1916
Miscellaneous	West Riding Brigade.		
Miscellaneous	Counter Battery Orders for Y day.		
Miscellaneous	Counter Battery Orders For Y (2) Day.	29/06/1916	29/06/1916
Miscellaneous	D/247	23/06/1916	23/06/1916
Miscellaneous			
Miscellaneous	Battery C/247		
Miscellaneous	Battery A/247		
Miscellaneous	Appendix D. Areas To Be Engaged With Gas Shell.		

121/5332

H.Q. Division

3rd W.R. Field Arty Bde

Vol I 1 — 31.5.15

Army Form C. 2118.

WAR DIARY
or
INTELLIGENCE SUMMARY.
(Erase heading not required.)

Instructions regarding War Diaries and Intelligence Summaries are contained in F. S. Regs., Part II. and the Staff Manual respectively. Title pages will be prepared in manuscript.

Place	Date	Hour	Summary of Events and Information	Remarks and references to Appendices
Fleurbaix	1915 May 1			
	2		Hostile aircraft active in early morning - signals dropped	
	3		Enemy shell FLEURBAIX - few rounds	
	7	3.10pm	Enemy shell FLEURBAIX - six rounds, three (which failed to burst.)	
	8		Wagon line moved to H.16.c.5.7. (Sheet 36 N.W./20000)	
			An "A" m moved to former position of wagon line	
	9		Attack on enemy's lines - firing opens at 5.0 am	
			Farm in rear of F.R. Battery on fire at 6.40 am - Officers' billet	
			Enemy shell FLEURBAIX 12.15 p.m. - 22 rounds 5.9 Howitzer	
			Shrapnel bursts over H.Q's dug-out 2.45 p.m.	
			Afternoon & evening quiet - no casualties.	
	10		Enemy shell FLEURBAIX at 5.15 am 10 rounds	
			" " " 6.30 pm 12 "	
	11		" " " 11.10 am 8 "	
			Hostile aeroplane over village 5.30 am flying low.	
			Wagon line moved to H.15.a.8.7. (Sheet 36 N.W. 1/20000)	

Army Form C. 2118.

WAR DIARY
or
INTELLIGENCE SUMMARY.
(Erase heading not required.)

Instructions regarding War Diaries and Intelligence Summaries are contained in F. S. Regs., Part II. and the Staff Manual respectively. Title pages will be prepared in manuscript.

Place	Date	Hour	Summary of Events and Information	Remarks and references to Appendices
FLEURBAIX	1915 May 12	8.30am	German aeroplane over FLEURBAIX	
			Enemy shell FLEURBAIX 4.50pm — 1 round	
	13		Quiet. all ration & water carts to be in dug outs by midnight	
	14	1 am	Artillery bombardment of German trenches until 1.20 am.	
			FLEURBAIX shelled at 2.15pm — 12 rounds	
	15	12.45pm	Artillery bombardment of enemy's trenches for 10 mins	
			Enemy shell FLEURBAIX — 6 rounds	
		4.45 am	Artillery bombardment repeated for 10 mins	
			Enemy shell FLEURBAIX — 5 rounds	
		8.45 am	Artillery bombardment repeated for 10 hours — No reply.	
	15/6	12 midnight	" " " " 5 " " "	
	17		All quiet — weather wet	
	18		Heavy rain all night — all quiet	
	19	11.15 am	FLEURBAIX shelled — 8 rounds	
	20,21,22,23		Normal	
	24	9 am	Enemy shell FLEURBAIX & trafr line — by shells over wagon line	

Army Form C. 2118.

WAR DIARY
or
INTELLIGENCE SUMMARY.
(Erase heading not required.)

Place	Date	Hour	Summary of Events and Information	Remarks and references to Appendices
FLEURBAIX	1915 May 24	8 pm	Bombardment of German trenches begins. Operations originally ordered for 8 pm on the 23rd inst. but postponed for 24 hours. The following Artillery took part in the offensive operations.	
			1st Br. R.F.A. Bgde.	
			3rd " R. F.A. "	
			4th " R (H) F.A. Bgde	
			3rd Highland (H) F.A. Bgde	
			5th Battery R.F.A.	
			36th " " "	
			55th (H) " " "	
			2 Batteries R.F.A. from 6th Div"	
			1 18 pr Bm for special purpose	
		8.20 pm	The 3rd Br. Bgde opened fire at 8.20 pm for 10 mins & bombarded the enemy's front trenches. Rate of fire 1 round per gun per minute	
		8.35 pm – 8.45 pm	All batteries repeat bombardment.	

Army Form C. 2118.

WAR DIARY
or
INTELLIGENCE SUMMARY.
(Erase heading not required.)

Instructions regarding War Diaries and Intelligence Summaries are contained in F. S. Regs., Part II. and the Staff Manual respectively. Title pages will be prepared in manuscript.

Place	Date	Hour	Summary of Events and Information	Remarks and references to Appendices
May 1915				
FLEURBAIX	25th	3.20am - 3.30am	Bombardment of enemy's front trench	
	26th		Enemy shell Bois Grenier & Rue d'Ancardie	
	28th		2/Lt S. E. Earnshaw arrives to relieve Major P.H. Wilson who is appointed to 4th Division	
	30th		Major P.H. Wilson departs to 4th Division	
	31st		Nomal	

1577 Wt.W10791/1773 500,000 1/15 D. E. & L. A.D.S.S./Forms/C. 2118.

49th Division

1/3rd W. R. Bde R.F.A.

Vol II 1 — 30.6.15.

101/599

a²
a/6.

WAR DIARY
or
INTELLIGENCE SUMMARY.
(Erase heading not required.)

Army Form C. 2118.

Place	Date	Hour	Summary of Events and Information	Remarks and references to Appendices
FLEURBAIX	1915 June 1		Major T.H. WALKER of the 1/4th E. ANGLIAN BGDE R.F.A.T. arrived from ENGLAND for 14 days course of instruction & is attached to 9th Battery.	
	2	5 pm	Enemy shell FLEURBAIX — 2 rounds	
	3	9.30 am	Hostile triplane over village	
	5	8.15 am	Two hostile aeroplanes over village — aerial activity displayed by the enemy throughout the day.	
	6	7.30 pm	7th Battery reported German infantry & cavalry moving N.E. in the direction of Bas Potières — not allowed to fire on them. Known by order of C.R.A.	
	7		Major T.H. Walker 4th E. ANGLIAN BGDE R.F.A. departed to the VIIIth Divn. Major R.A. Hatton & Lieut J.P.M. Hibbert of 2nd E.A. Bgde arrive for a 6 Shells [Course — are attached to 8th & 7th Batteries respy]	
	8	5 pm	FLEURBAIX shelled	
	11	5 pm	Hostile aeroplanes active	
	12	4 pm	FLEURBAIX shelled	
	13	2.30 pm	FLEURBAIX shelled	
	14	11.30 am	Shells bursting behind FLEURBAIX. Major Gainsford departed on leave Capt W. Howson assumes Temp: Command of 9th Battery A.J.C.	

Army Form C. 2118.

WAR DIARY
or
INTELLIGENCE SUMMARY.
(Erase heading not required.)

Instructions regarding War Diaries and Intelligence
Summaries are contained in F.S. Regs., Part II.
and the Staff Manual respectively. Title pages
will be prepared in manuscript.

Place	Date	Hour	Summary of Events and Information	Remarks and references to Appendices
FLEURBAIX	1915 June 17		Ammunition Column move to G.10.6.12. (Sheet 36 N.W. 1/20000)	
	18,19		Enemy aircraft active	
	20		From HQrs of 1st WR RFA R.G.A. shelled & burnt out.	Lieut. H. Gr. Thorne admitted to hospital
	21	11.30am	FLEURBAIX shelled	
	22,23,24		All quiet	Sheet 36 N.W. 1/20000
	25		Heavy thunderstorm during afternoon - torrential rainfall.	
	26/27	9.15pm	7th Battery & one section of 9th Battery move to camps at G.2.6.19. & G.2.6.6.5. (7th battery) & G.3.a.5.6. (9th battery) 7th Battery relieved by two sections 32nd Battery	
			9th " one " " 36th "	
	27/28	9.15pm	Remaining section of 9th Battery move to G.3.a.5.6.	
			8th Battery move to G.3.a.7.4 relieved by 33rd battery	
	28	6am	Headquarters move to G.2.6.7.8.	
	29	6pm	Brigade marches independently to Centre via NEUF BERQUIN. VIEUX BERQUIN, STRAZEELE & is housed outside the town	W.C.

1577 Wt. W10791/1773 500,000 1/15 D. D. & L.   A.D.S.S./Forms/C. 2118.

Army Form C. 2118.

WAR DIARY

~~INTELLIGENCE SUMMARY~~

(Erase heading not required.)

Place	Date	Hour	Summary of Events and Information	Remarks and references to Appendices
CAESTRE	June 30	9 pm	Brigade marches independently to billeting area E. J. WATOU via EECKE - STEENWOORDE - S. COO vredo - DROGLANDT - WATOU.	A/C

12/6272

49th Division

3nd W.R. Bde R.F.A.

Vol III

1-31-4-15

Army Form C. 2118.

WAR DIARY
or
INTELLIGENCE SUMMARY.
(Erase heading not required.)

Place	Date	Hour	Summary of Events and Information	Remarks and references to Appendices
WATOU	1915 July 1st		Brigade in rest area E. of WATOU.	
	2	4.40pm	Inspection of 147th Infantry Brigade, 3rd West Riding Brigade R.F.A. & 2nd Field Ambulance by the Army Commander General Sir H.C. Plumer.	
	3,4,5,6.		Brigade in rest area	
	7	6.20pm	7th Battery complete, one section each of 8th & 9th Batteries & Ints Ammunition Column moved to new positions	
			7th Battery at B.22.d.1.8. Sheet 28. N.W. 1/20000	
			8th " " B.16.a.9.2. " " "	
			9th " " B.15.b.8.7. " " "	
			Am. Col. " A.23.d.E.7. " " "	
	8		Registration of enemy's trenches commenced. Zone B.12.b.6.2 to C.13.b.5.10.	
ELVERDINGHE		9.0 am	Headquarters, remaining sections of batteries & remainder of Am. Col. moved into new positions.	
	9	10 am	Brigade relieved 32nd Brigade R.F.A. & took over their H.Q. Qrs at B.15.d.4.8. Sheet 28 N.W. 1/20000	

WAR DIARY
or
INTELLIGENCE SUMMARY.
(Erase heading not required.)

Army Form C. 2118.

Place	Date	Hour	Summary of Events and Information	Remarks and references to Appendices
ELVERDINGHE	1915 July 9		One section each of the 27th, 134th & 135th Batteries 32nd Brigade known attached to the 7th, 9th & 8th Batteries respectively. Wagon lines H.Qrs at B.20.a.f.7. 7th Battery B.14.c.2.3. 8th " B.14.a.5.5. 9th " B.19.c.9.3.	
	10	8.40pm	Brigade called upon by G.O.C. 148th Inf. Bde for Artillery fire. The G.O.C. stated that the Germans had made the left sector of his Brigade afterwards reported by our liaison officer as C.7.c.5.2. Within 2 minutes of receiving message 9th Battery opened fire followed by 8th & 7th. All 18 per guns attacked took part
		9.20pm	trench reported re-captured & all batteries lifted their fire on to Communication trenches.
		10.30pm	ordered to stop firing & stand fast. Close communication was kept with our liaison officer. The French Group under Major de Trestane offered their services

WAR DIARY or INTELLIGENCE SUMMARY

Army Form C. 2118.

Place	Date	Hour	Summary of Events and Information	Remarks and references to Appendices
ELVERDINGHE	1915 July 10	cont	and stood ready to create a barrage at C.1.c.7.2. & where required. Rounds fired 15 pdr & 18 pdr. 7th Battery 27 rounds. 6th 364 rounds. 9th 190 rounds. Casualties - nil.	Sheet 28. P.M. 1/20000
	11	About 11.15 am F.O.O. 9th Battery reported enemy apparently massing in trenches about C.7.c.3.9. — 12 rounds fired by 9th Battery with considerable effect. Further infantry were observed in same place during afternoon when 12 more rounds were fired. Telegram re. 2nd Army Commander desires to command prompt action if troops seen "Dug in" when attacked last night. Registration continued. 9th Battery fire on German working party. 7th & 8th batteries' morning stations shelled.	
	12			
	13	3.30 pm.	9th Battery fire on German working party. Further registration carried out. 9th Battery F.O.O. reports small party of men in enemy trench in front of farm 14. 9th Battery fired a salvo on the trench.	

Army Form C. 2118.

WAR DIARY
or
INTELLIGENCE SUMMARY.
(Erase heading not required.)

Place	Date	Hour	Summary of Events and Information	Remarks and references to Appendices
ELVERDINGHE	1915 July 13	8.15	Immediately afterwards a heavy bombardment of our trenches commenced. They also fired on the French trenches S. of the Railway. The whole of the Divisional Arty. then replied from that time until dark, smoke reduced observation impossible.	
		8.30	Batteries ordered to fire on German Communication trenches at a slow rate. 7th Battery reported S.O.S. message rec'd. to that effect.	
		8.43	7th Battery Section fire 20 secs. Firing reported excellent by Liaison Officer.	
		8.53	Batteries ordered section fire 10 secs.	
		8.59	Reported that Germans have captured part of 4th York Han C. trenches on left	
		9.2	Infantry holding their own & pushing up reinforcements	
		9.7	Farm 14 reported destroyed by our fire.	
		9.22	Reported that Germans have made large hole in 4th Y & L trench with heavy shell but we are bombing them out.	
		9.25	7th Battery report hits on guns on fire.	

WAR DIARY
or
INTELLIGENCE SUMMARY.
(Erase heading not required.)

Army Form C. 2118.

Place	Date	Hour	Summary of Events and Information	Remarks and references to Appendices
ELVERDINGHE	1915 July 13	9.27pm	7th Battery report red rockets over German trenches Batteries ordered "section fire 30 secs".	
		9.38pm	Four shells burst round Hd.Qrs. Gas shells bursting near 8th Battery.	
		10.2p	C.R.A ordered fire to slacken down gradually but not to cease. Section fire 1 minute.	
		10.15p	18 pdrs ordered to "Cease fire" - Ammunition getting short.	
		10.20p	Batteries stop firing - one section ordered to stand by.	
	14		Major Ferguson "A" Battery 46th Brigade R.F.A. reported at 6 p.m. One section of this battery attached to S.R. & one to 9th Battery & relieved sections of 32nd Brigade which rejoined their Brigade. Bde. Am. Colmn moved to A15 a begon lines moved to A.17.d.9.2. also wagon lines of "A" Bty attached.	Sheet 28 N.W. 1/20000

WAR DIARY or INTELLIGENCE SUMMARY

Army Form C. 2118.

Place	Date	Hour	Summary of Events and Information	Remarks and references to Appendices
ELVERDINGHE	1915 July 15		8th Battery wagon line moved to A.17.c.2.5. & "A" Battery wagon line to A.17.c.8.4. Amm: Colm A.9.a.9.2. Batteries registered.	
		8.52pm	S.O.S. Call from 146th Inf. Bgde.	
		8.57	Fired on FORTIN 17 by Int. orders. Infantry report firing short. Batteries increased range 100 yds — section fire 20 secs. Infantry report still firing short — range increased another 100 yds & in response to a third appeal yet another 100 yds.	
		9.20	Batteries stop fire & stand fast. Later "Cease firing". No casualties. 7th Battery 62 rounds fired 18 pdrs 56 rounds 8th " 86 " " 9th " 63 " "	
	16	6.15am	Heavy shelling near 9th Battery with gas shells. Remainder of day quiet — weather very bad.	

WAR DIARY or INTELLIGENCE SUMMARY

Army Form C. 2118.

Place	Date	Hour	Summary of Events and Information	Remarks and references to Appendices
ELVERDINGHE	1915 July 17		Moved Hd.Qrs. to Brewery B15c.6.5. Amⁿ Colⁿ moved to A21.6.6.3.	
	18		ELVERDINGHE shelled during morning - windmill set on fire. Hostile aeroplanes very active.	
		7.20pm	Liason officer reports enemy visible in skirmishing order at C7. c.7.9.	
		7.24pm	8th. 9th & A/46th Batteries ordered to open fire on the front	
		7.41pm	7th Battery opened fire on communication trenches running from FARM 14 & Corpst to the right.	
		7.28	A/46th Battery cease fire. 8th Battery ordered to "cease fire".	
		7.35	8th Battery open fire on communication trenches & covered country. 7th Section fire 20 fccc.	
		7.37	Hd.Q^{rs} R.A. report Zeppelin going N. from S. of VARNELLES	
		7.39	Infantry ask for increased rate of fire. 9th Battery ordered "Section fire 10 fccc".	

Army Form C. 2118.

WAR DIARY
or
INTELLIGENCE SUMMARY.
(Erase heading not required.)

Instructions regarding War Diaries and Intelligence Summaries are contained in F. S. Regs., Part II. and the Staff Manual respectively. Title pages will be prepared in manuscript.

Place	Date	Hour	Summary of Events and Information	Remarks and references to Appendices
ELVERDINGHE	1915 July 18	7.45	7th 8th & 9th Batteries increase their range by 100 yds - by order	
		7.44	of Infantry	
		7.46	9th Battery increase further 200 yds	
			"Cease fire" issued by —	
			Ammunition expended 7th Battery 48 rounds	
			8th " 70 "	
			9th " 55 "	
			A/46th 21 "	
	19		Enemy search for anti aircraft gun - many shells fall near A/46th battery. German aeroplanes very active.	
	20		A/46th Battery shelled - direct hit on Bipods late H.Q.??	
	21		A/46th Battery again shelled - farm buildings hit. ELVERDINGHE shelled 8.30am to 10.30am - have set on fire 100 yds N. of 9th Battery to village.	
		7pm	9th Battery dispersed a working party at C.7.c.2.10.	R.L.

Army Form C. 2118.

WAR DIARY
or
INTELLIGENCE SUMMARY.
(Erase heading not required.)

Place	Date	Hour	Summary of Events and Information	Remarks and references to Appendices
ELVERDINGHE	1915 July 22		A/46 Battery & farm shelled – barn hit three times otherwise no damage	
	23	4.50am	Infantry reported working party at the redoubt of the new German trench at C7 c.2.10. 9th Battery fired four rounds into them	
	24		German aeroplanes active in evening, otherwise quiet. One aeroplane reported hit.	
	25		Morning quiet – aeroplanes very active in evening. At 6.45 pm a German aeroplane was seen to fall in our lines in the direction of YPRES. Having been shot down by one of ours. Registration continued by A/46 Battery.	
	26		ELVERDINGHE shelled 10.30 am to 12 midday. Several shells failed to burst totally four shells in quick succession	

Army Form C. 2118.

WAR DIARY
or
INTELLIGENCE SUMMARY.
(Erase heading not required.)

Place	Date	Hour	Summary of Events and Information	Remarks and references to Appendices
ELVERDINGHE	1915 July 27		ELVERDINGHE shelled at midday and 5 p.m. - Several blind shells.	
	28		9th Battery registered. A/46th Battery fired 12 rounds into communication trenches at FARM 14 at request of Infantry H.Q.	
		6.45 p.m	9th Battery heavily shelled - 77 large shells falling round the position. One section move into new position at B15.a.7.2	B: Broadhurst wounded slight
	29		9th Battery fired 12 rounds into Communication trench behind FARM 14 at request of Infantry Brigade	
	30		9th Battery continue registration. A/46th Battery fire on working party into front road.	
			H.Q. moved to B15.c.2.7. (28 N.W. 1/20000)	
	31	7 p.m	A/46th Battery shelled with gas shells. The gas was distinctly noticeable for 3 or 4 hrs afterwards within a 400 yds radius of the bursts.	

J.E. Earnshaw Capt & Adjt
for O.C. 13th W.R. R.F.A.

R.F.

121/6754

49th Division

1/3rd W.R. Bde R.F.A.
Vol IV
August 15

War Diary for August 1915

3rd West Riding Brigade
R.F.A.T.

Army Form C. 2118

WAR DIARY
or
INTELLIGENCE SUMMARY.
(Erase heading not required.)

Instructions regarding War Diaries and Intelligence Summaries are contained in F. S. Regs., Part II. and the Staff Manual respectively. Title pages will be prepared in manuscript.

Place	Date	Hour	Summary of Events and Information	Remarks and references to Appendices
ELVERDINGHE	1915 August 1		9R Battery fired on German working party — 12 rounds. " " " evacuating farm at C.8.a.7.2. After it had been set on fire by 4R Siege Battery.	
	2		9R Battery fired no rounds at working party which dispersed.	
	3		Our heavy batteries commenced firing at 10pm for an hour. Enemy replied with light heavy guns at 11.10 for about half an hour.	
	4		Day quiet – weather too bad for aerial observation. 9R Battery forward position shelled at 6.30pm — 12 rounds.	
	5		8R Battery engaged enemy battery at C.8.6.5.1. 9R " fired on working party about TOOTHPICK FARM C.7.6.9.2. A/46 — silenced a trench mortar at repeat of infantry.	13 rounds
	6	6am	8R Battery fired on working party. Retaliation points registered. Heavy shelling during night on both sides.	

Army Form C. 2118.

WAR DIARY
or
INTELLIGENCE SUMMARY.
(Erase heading not required.)

Instructions regarding War Diaries and Intelligence Summaries are contained in F. S. Regs., Part II. and the Staff Manual respectively. Title pages will be prepared in manuscript.

Place	Date	Hour	Summary of Events and Information	Remarks and references to Appendices
ELVERDINGHE	1915 August 7		Working party fired on. Ground in vicinity of Brigade H.Q. shelled during afternoon. Heavy shelling during night on both sides.	
	8		9th Battery heavily shelled between 2.0 & 2.30 am. One man was wounded and died shortly afterwards in hospital. Heavy shelling on both sides during the day.	
		6.30 p.m.	Bombardment of enemy's trenches by 49th Divl Arty, 46th Bgde R.F.A. and French mortars and howitzers assisted by the French 45th Divl Arty. Object - Demolition of on left of British line to cover attack by 6th Division in the vicinity of HOOGE in order to recapture ground recently lost.	LEFT GROUP. 7th Battery 8th " 9th " Aph "
		6.30 p.m.	Wire cutting by Left Group less 7th HR Battery. Two rounds per gun per minute (Shrapnel)	
		6.45	Enemy retaliate on trenches & batteries	
		7.0	1st phase ceases. French artillery open fire on German front line trenches	
		7.5	A/46 wire reported cut also Dinenmel wire (telephone)	

Army Form C. 2118.

WAR DIARY
or
INTELLIGENCE SUMMARY.
(Erase heading not required.)

Place	Date	Hour	Summary of Events and Information	Remarks and references to Appendices
ELVERDINGHE	1915 August 8.	7.10 p	Germans reported by 9th Battery to be massing in redoubt S. of FARM 14.	
		7.18 p	French fire on redoubt with successful results. Left Group held in readiness to repel any counter attacks and in the interregnum (7pm to 10pm) batteries "in a position of observation".	
		7.29	German Captive balloon pulled down. This balloon was reported to have been sent up 10 mins before bombardment commenced.	
		7.57	9th Battery fire a few rounds into FARM 14.	
		8.1 p	Communication reestablished with Divisional H.Qrs.	
		8.20 p	S.O.S. call received from 147th Inf. Bgde. — 6 rounds fired.	
		8.33 p	S.O.S. cancelled.	
		9.45 p	Communication reestablished with A/46th Battery. Hay report 1 man killed and 1 wounded.	

Army Form C. 2118.

WAR DIARY
or
INTELLIGENCE SUMMARY.
(Erase heading not required.)

Instructions regarding War Diaries and Intelligence Summaries are contained in F. S. Regs., Part II. and the Staff Manual respectively. Title pages will be prepared in manuscript.

Place	Date	Hour	Summary of Events and Information	Remarks and references to Appendices
ELVERDINGHE	1915 August 8	10.0 pm	All batteries in LEFT GROUP fire 1 salvo each on front trenches	
		10.15 pm	Salvos repeated	
	9	12.30 am	Programme repeated	2/Lt C.D. BIRKS joined 4th posted
		10 pm		
		12.40 am	One salvo per battery on second line trenches and communication to Am. Col.	
		12.45 am	Salvos repeated	
	10		Brigade Casualties — nil.	
		9.25 am	Infantry called for support — 8th & 19th Batteries fired on second line trenches. 7th & 9th Batteries fire on working parties.	
	11		9th Battery fire on workers party. A/46th Battery retaliated to German fire at 4.0 p.m. & fired on FARM 14. 9th Batty remaining section move to B15a.7.2.	Lieut M.J. Hunter
	12		All batteries fire in retaliation — 3 rounds each.	
	13		Further registration by A/46 Battery — Enemy quiet weather unfavourable for observation purposes.	invalided to England and struck off the Strength
	14	F.2m	9th Battery refire from new position. All batteries retaliate at 4.47 pm in response to Infy call. Heavy shelling in evening by enemy on our heavy batteries.	

Army Form C. 2118.

WAR DIARY
or
INTELLIGENCE SUMMARY.
(Erase heading not required.)

Place	Date	Hour	Summary of Events and Information	Remarks and references to Appendices
ELVERDINGHE	1915 Aug. 15		Quiet.	2nd Lieut. E.G. Rice admitted to hospital
	16		Enemy shell all round ELVERDINGHE. at intervals during the morning. 9th Battery replied at several points. Enemy artillery very active - found to right of 2nd Battery shelled heavily (B.16.d.) German aeroplanes over during the evening.	
	17			
	18	1.15pm	Enemy started shelling all round Sper. H.Qrs with gas shells & shrapnel. One gas shell struck the house. One was of 31st Hy. Batty. & one was of 20th Siege Batt. wounded. About 30 rounds fired. ELVERDINGHE was shelled late in the afternoon. About 6.30 pm the enemy shelled a French battery on the right of 146 Battery firing a great many heavy shells 37 of which were counted "blind". The number fired shot in spite of the accuracy of the fire, most of the shells falling in the battery, not a man or gun was injured. The shells fired were 5.9" and 8".	Lieut S.J. Slake admitted to hospital

A.C.
160.

Army Form C. 2118.

WAR DIARY
or
INTELLIGENCE SUMMARY.
(Erase heading not required.)

Place	Date	Hour	Summary of Events and Information	Remarks and references to Appendices
ELVERDINGHE	Aug. 1918 18		A/46 Battery fired one salvo on KIEL COTTAGE and one on CROSSROADS at C.1.c.8.1. (about 28 N.W. Town). 7th & 9th Batteries did not fire. ELVERDINGHE shelled intermittently during the day.	Capt G.N FOWLER joins the Bgde and is posted to 9th Battery
	19	9.1am	Order to retaliate received from 148th Inf. Bgde. All batteries fired three rounds each on retaliation points.	
	20	2.11pm 3.57pm	Retaliation order from 147th Infy Bgde. Batteries fire three rounds each. Second Retaliation order from 147th Inf Bgde. Batteries again fire three rounds each. 9th Battery fired 16 rounds at working party round TOOTHPICK FARM. Three German Observation Balloons reported up - one close behind their lines. ELVERDINGHE shelled at 5.15 pm. Enemy aeroplanes very active in the early morning	

WAR DIARY
or
INTELLIGENCE SUMMARY.

Army Form C. 2118.

Place	Date	Hour	Summary of Events and Information	Remarks and references to Appendices
ELVERDINGHE	1915 Aug. 21	1.39am	Received "Test F.32" Batteries fired 1.41 am. A receipt of message "Test" batteries immediately fire on pre-arranged points in the Section of trench ordered. One round per battery. Day quiet - too misty for observation.	
		7.30pm	Enemy shelled 9.R Battery's old position & the vicinity with 5.9" and 8" shells. About 100 rounds fired.	
	22		Enemy aeroplanes very active in early morning for battery-spotting at mid-day - 25 to 30 shells - no damage.	
		4.55pm	Order to retaliate received from 147th hy. Bde. All batteries fired 4.56 pm. Retaliation order again received at 6.44pm. All fired at 6.45pm. 9.R Battery fired 20 rounds on working parties round Toetjesch[?] Farm (c.7.6.9.2.)	
	23	10pm	Retaliation order received from 147th hy Bde. Fired 1.12pm. 15 shells were fired into ELVERDINGHE at 1.15pm but no one hurt.	

Army Form C. 2118.

WAR DIARY
or
INTELLIGENCE SUMMARY.
(Erase heading not required.)

Instructions regarding War Diaries and Intelligence Summaries are contained in F. S. Regs., Part II. and the Staff Manual respectively. Title pages will be prepared in manuscript.

Place	Date	Hour	Summary of Events and Information	Remarks and references to Appendices
ELVERDINGHE	1915 August 24		At 8.42am ant bry fire received orders to retaliate 5th Battery fired a salvo at a working party at C.2.C.3.2. 9th " fired 4 rounds on working party at TOOTHPICK FARM. Morning very quiet. Weather misty and observation difficult. Enemy shelled BOESINGHE during the afternoon	
	25		Retaliation call received from Infantry at 4.30am. three rounds fired per battery. 9th Battery fired eight rounds on working party at TOOTHPICK FARM and nine rounds at working party at LAKE FARM. A.46 Battery fired three salvos on working party E. of FARM 14 and one salvo on KEL COTTAGE.	
	26		8th & 9th Batteries reported several points in enemy lines. Hostile aeroplanes very active throughout the day. Batteries "stood by" ready to open fire from 5.30 pm to 7.11 pm in	A.C.

WAR DIARY
or
INTELLIGENCE SUMMARY.
(Erase heading not required.)

Army Form C. 2118.

Place	Date	Hour	Summary of Events and Information	Remarks and references to Appendices
ELVERDINGHE	1915 Aug 25	5.30 p	in accordance with Operation Orders attached	Capt N HOWSON to be MAJOR. Lieut M J HUNTER to be CAPTAIN. 2nd Lt R C BENSON to be LIEUT. to date from July 15, 1915
	26	7.23 p.m	Retaliation from Infantry Bgde Hd Qrs — all fired 7.23 p.m.	
	27		9" Battery fired five rounds in registration. P/4/6 Battery fired one dud round at Q.2.a.10.8.9 also one round	2/Lt R G ROE reverted to England and struck off strength of Brigade Sept
		3.30 p	particular. Two German aeroplanes took a look at the whole of our front without interruption. Shortly afterwards our troops trenches were heavily shelled with S.G. shells. 9" Battery's gun position very heavily shelled during the day	
	28		Retaliation round fired by all batteries at 3.45 pm & 6.36 p.m in response to calls from Infantry Bgde. H.Q.rs 9" Battery's gun position heavily shelled again during the day	2/Lt R E YATES taken on Brigade strength and posted to 9" Battery
		7.30 p	9" Battery fired two rounds at working party at PILKEM CROSS.	

Army Form C. 21

WAR DIARY
or
INTELLIGENCE SUMMARY.
(Erase heading not required.)

Instructions regarding War Diaries and Intelligence Summaries are contained in F. S. Regs., Part II. and the Staff Manual respectively. Title pages will be prepared in manuscript.

Place	Date	Hour	Summary of Events and Information	Remarks and references to Appendices
ELVERDINGHE	1915 Aug. 29		Enemy's artillery very active during the morning. BOESINGHE shelled heavily with 5.9. Afternoon dull and very quiet.	
	30		7" Battery fired twice. 8" Battery fired twice. 9" & 1.2" Battery fired twice & 9.46 once in retaliation during the afternoon. None made last time. 9" Battery fired 8 rounds on working party at TOOTHPICK FARM (C.7.f.102) Trench mortars very active on both sides during the afternoon. Enemy shelled CHASSEUR FARM 9" Battery and 9.46 Battery positions. Post, one man of 9.46 Battery being killed. Another O.P. of the 9" Battery was shelled during the day at B12.c.9.9.	
	31		7" Battery fired two rounds on working party at PLOTEN CROSS Shelters. Fired twice on working parties at the same place. 9.46 Battery fired on parties at ZOUAVE and TOOTHPICK FARMS. BOESINGHE very heavy shelled. ELVERDINGHE shelled at 5.pm.	

No......

OPERATION ORDERS

by

Lieut. Colonel Charles Clifford, V.D., R.F.A.(T)
Commanding Left Group.

25th August 1915.

Reference BOESINGHE Map 1/10,000.

INTENTION. At 5.30.p.m. today an attempt will be made by the \ BRITISH / FRENCH and BELGIAN aeroplanes to fire the forest of HOULTHULST. The Heavy Artillery have orders to participate.

It is suspect possible that the enemy's artillery may retaliate. The attached scheme is for necessary action in due course.

Orders will be issued from this office when you are to open fire.

Should you have direct call from the Infantry, the usual Retaliation Scheme is to be employed.

TASKS.	OBJECTIVES.	REMARKS.	ROUNDS PER GUN PER MINUTE.
LEFT GROUP. (less A/46 Bty)			
7th Battery.	C 7 d 2.8 to C 7 d 5.8	Commence with salvo and thence search up and down with single rounds and pause of 10 minutes to be allowed, so that enemy will leave cover.	1 round per gun per 2 minutes for 5 minutes.
8th Battery.	FARM 14 to C 7 central	-do-	-do-
9th Battery.	C 7 a 3.8 to C 7 b 2.2	-do-	-do-
A/46 Battery.	To stand by for orders.		

Lieut. Colonel. V.D., R.F.A.(T)
Commandg. 1/3rd West Rid. Bde R.F.A.(T).

Issued at 5.15.p.m.

1669/121

49th Division

1/3rd W. R. Bde R.F.A.

Vol V

Sept. 15

War Diary.

1/10 West Lab. Fus. A.T.M.T.
49th (W.R.) Division

Septr 1916.

WAR DIARY
or
INTELLIGENCE SUMMARY.
(Erase heading not required.)

Army Form C. 2118.

Place	Date	Hour	Summary of Events and Information	Remarks and references to Appendices
ELVERDINGHE	19/15 Sept			
	1.		All batteries fired in retaliation at 3.33 p.m. in response to callo from 148th Infy Brigade. A/46 Battery fired 13 rounds at C.1.a.9.8. in cooperation with aeroplane & 9th Battery one round.	
	2		Each battery turned one gun to forward position. 7th 8th 19th Batteries registering forward guns with Retaliation rounds fired at 2.55 pm & 4.38 pm	
			9th Battery fired 8 rounds at Battery to rear of TOOTHPICK FARM at C.F.6.5.2. 8th Battery O.P. at TUGELA FARM B16.b.35. wrecked by H.E. shell. Enemy artillery very active throughout the day.	
	3		9th Battery fired 11 rounds in registration of forward gun. 3 Rounds fired on working party at EOLIAN FARM C.F. c.2.5. Observation difficult owing to mist.	
	4	10.5 am	All batteries fired two rounds each in retaliation. 7th Battery continued registration. Enemy shelled BOESINGHE.	

WAR DIARY
or
INTELLIGENCE SUMMARY.

Army Form C. 2118.

Place	Date	Hour	Summary of Events and Information	Remarks and references to Appendices
ELVERDINGHE	1915 Sept. 4	7.25pm	All batteries fired 3 rounds each in retaliation. Heavy ransfade during last three days	
	5		A/46 Battery fired on two working parties at C7.c.5.8. and on one at FARM 14. – 20 rounds fired. Fresh on no left bombarded the German lines during the greater part of the afternoon. Supposed by our heavy batteries. Enemy retaliated on the BOESINGHE – ELVERDINGHE road. 6" Battery fired 10 rounds on working parties observed at FARM 14 (Trench map). Fired me rounds in north eastern of registration of forward gun.	
	6		Ft Battery registered forward gun on trenches in front of EOLIAN FARM C7.c.2.4. A/46 Battery fired 26 rounds at screen observed at C7.C.10.4. Enemy shelled canal bank and BOESINGHE during the afternoon.	2/Lt Elliott Jr Battery wounded rifle bullet

Army Form C. 2118

WAR DIARY
or
INTELLIGENCE SUMMARY.
(Erase heading not required.)

Place	Date	Hour	Summary of Events and Information	Remarks and references to Appendices
ELVERDINGHE	1915 Sept 7		All batteries fired in retaliation at 4.15pm. 6th and 9th Batteries fired on working parties observed during the day. A 5.6 fried 12 rounds at German aeroplane which fell just behind their lines at C.7.d.6.7. Misty all day - observation difficult. Two officers arrive from England on 14 days Course of Instruction.	2/Lt P.R. CAMPBELL 159th R.F.A to 9th Batty. 2/Lt H.C. HOLDER 157th Bde RFA to 6th Batty 2/Lt HUGHBREWITT 152nd Bde RFA to 9th Batty 2/Lt P.S. RAWSON 152nd Bde RFA to 446 Batty
	8		9th Battery fired in cooperation with aeroplane on targets at C7.6.94 and C.6.6.42. Several working parties observed and fired on. ELVERDINGHE shelled at 3.30 pm	
	9		Retaliation called for three times by 146th Infy. Brigade. A/46 Battery fired two rounds at trench mortar at C.7.c.5.8 at request of Infy. ELVERDINGHE CHÂTEAU shelled at 6.15pm.	
	10		All batteries retaliated five times during the day. German artillery very active all day. Aeroplanes constantly over.	

Army Form C. 2118

WAR DIARY
or
INTELLIGENCE SUMMARY.
(Erase heading not required.)

Place	Date	Hour	Summary of Events and Information	Remarks and references to Appendices
ELVERDINGHE	1915 Sept 11		All batteries retaliated six times at report by F.S.S.H. 6th Battery registered trenches at C.7.a.6.5. and C.7.b.2.6. German howitzer battery fired about 200 rounds into a house at B10.d.9.9. Several German working parties fired on during the day.	26 NW/20000
	12.		All batteries retaliated nine times at request by F.S.S.H. Great activity on part of German aircraft. One aeroplane flew over 7th Battery. Have a sort of exchange whistle having a shell penetrated hole immediately after two in. heard an enemy battery fire two rounds from right front of 7th Battery's position. Received orders to cooperate with 4th Siege Battery in bombardment of enemy's front trench from C.7.c.7 to C.7.c.7. Task allotted — to open fire on any of the enemy batteries on tracks by 4th Siege Battery. No enemy observed today.	

WAR DIARY
or
INTELLIGENCE SUMMARY.

Army Form C. 2118

Place	Date	Hour	Summary of Events and Information	Remarks and references to Appendices
ELVERDINGHE	1915 Sept 12		So fire not opened.	
	13	9 p.m.	BOESINGHE heavily shelled. One section of 42nd battery R.F.A. relieved one section of 144.6 battery. All batteries in Left Group returned fire twice during the day. 7th and 9th batteries fired in working parties at C.P.C. 1.4.	
			Section of 42nd battery registered several points in enemy's line & their trenches.	
		9 p.m.	Another section of 42nd battery relieved the remaining section of A/46 battery who rejoined their Brigade. One section of 42nd battery in rest area.	
	14		7th battery fired three salvos on working party at C.P.C.0.5 and dispersed them.	
			9th battery registered registration screens on enemy's parapet at C.P. a.5.7.	
			9th battery continued registration of forward gun.	
			42nd battery registered further points in enemy's trenches.	

WAR DIARY
or
INTELLIGENCE SUMMARY.
(Erase heading not required.)

Army Form C. 2118

Place	Date	Hour	Summary of Events and Information	Remarks and references to Appendices
ELVERDINGHE	1915 Sept 14		Enemy shelled BOESINGHE during morning - two 5.9 batteries fired from the direction of PILCKEM	Ref sheet 28 N.W. Ypres
		3.30	Between 25 and 30 shells were fired round ELVERDINGHE Several failed shell.	
	15		Morning very quiet - heavy mist prevented observation Enemy shelled BOESINGHE CHATEAU and trenches in vicinity	
		3pm	ELVERDINGHE shelled at 1.0 pm 17 minutes fired of which 5 were blind.	
	16		7th Battery fired on working parties at C.8.20.4 and at PILKEMCROSS C.2.c.6.3 8th Battery fired on working parties at C.9.b.8.3 and C.9.b.9.1. also rifished trench at C.8.a.S.8. 9th Battery 6 rounds fired by aeroplane observation on C.1.c.8.1. 42nd Battery continued registration of enemy's trenches	

Army Form C. 2118

WAR DIARY
or
INTELLIGENCE SUMMARY.
(Erase heading not required.)

Instructions regarding War Diaries and Intelligence Summaries are contained in F. S. Regs., Part II and the Staff Manual respectively. Title pages will be prepared in manuscript.

Place	Date	Hour	Summary of Events and Information	Remarks and references to Appendices
ELVERDINGE	1915 Sept 17		Morning quiet - enemy shelled ELVERDINGHE and vicinity (40 to 50 shells) from 1pm to 2.30 pm and again at 4.30 pm with heavy shells (about 25 rounds) 42nd Battery fired on crossroads at C2.c.5.7 and C1.c.8.1 also a gun position at C1.d.1.7 by aeroplane observation. 42 A battery position (B15.a.5.7) was shelled by 4.2 battery - 15 rounds	
	18		ELVERDINGHE lightly shelled. 9th Battery engaged target at C2.c.5.7 and fired 10 rounds by aeroplane observation. 9th Battery fired at C1.d.1.7 by aeroplane observation. Noticeable increase in the activity of enemy's artillery during the last few days. All batteries of retaliated at 5.30 pm	
	19		9th Battery fired on C1.c.8.1 by aeroplane observation. Hostile aeroplanes very active in the morning. Enemy shelled all round ELVERDINGHE - shooting was very wild.	

WAR DIARY or INTELLIGENCE SUMMARY

Army Form C. 2118

Place	Date	Hour	Summary of Events and Information	Remarks and references to Appendices
ELVERDINGHE	1915 Sept 20		The four officers attached for 10 days course of instruction left for England to rejoin their brigades. Very heavy shelling by enemy throughout the day. 7th Battery fired 6 rounds on working party at C8.a.16. 9th " " by aeroplane observation on cross roads at C1.c.8.1. 42nd " " fire on working party behind screen at C8.a.7.6. ELVERDINGHE and ELVERDINGHE — BRIELEN road shelled intermittently during the day.	
	21		8th Battery registered a supposed battery at C1.d.16. One section of C/63rd Battery relieved one section of 42nd Battery.	
	22	4 pm	Relief of 42nd Battery by C Battery 63rd Bde completed. 11th W.R. Battery (Howitzer) attached to Left Group. Bombardment of Left Group Zone. Object of the bombardment to annoy the enemy and induce	

WAR DIARY
or
INTELLIGENCE SUMMARY.

(Erase heading not required.)

Army Form C. 2118

Place	Date	Hour	Summary of Events and Information	Remarks and references to Appendices
ELVERDINGHE	1915 Sept 22		reply and few bursts as many flashes as possible for future use. The front to be observed being that covered by squares C.2, C.9, and C.16 (28 N.W.) snowy. Expenditure of ammunition limited to 9 rounds per gun. Bombardment finished at 5 p.m. No reply from enemy.	
	23		Retaliation recently received from 9th Brigade 12.43 p.m all batteries fired one round each. 9th Battery fired 13 rounds by aeroplane observation at C.1.c.8.1. Lieut General Sir Th. Kier, K.C.B. inspected wagon lines and Amn Coln	
	24.		Quiet day – weather misty and wet.	

Place	Date	Hour	Summary of Events and Information	Remarks and references to Appendices
EVERDINGHE	1915 Sept 25		Demonstration carried out by 6th Corps. - ordered to commence at 4.20 am but postponed for one hour. Tasks allotted to Left Group :- 1st Phase 4.20 am to 4.56 am 9th Hr Battery 4.20 to 4.56 am to flick area B12.b.6.7 & C7.d.1.3 To watch hostile battery at C9.c.16 and counter it if it opens fire. - 22 rounds allotted shrapnel. 5" - - " To flick area C2.c. 28 rounds shrapnel C/63rd Battery - 2nd hr. line tench C7d.5.8 to C7.b.6.3 and factory to OSCAR FARM and watch hostile battery at C8.b.4.2 and counter it if it opens fire. 60 rounds shrapnel 7R Battery front line tench C7.b.9.1 to C7a.6.1. 20 rounds 1R (How) Battery Bombard C.F. C.1.3 EOLIAN FARM. C7d.5.8 and C7 central. - 50 rounds H.E. At 4.56 am Gas was to be turned on against hostile trenches	

WAR DIARY or INTELLIGENCE SUMMARY

Army Form C. 2118

Place	Date	Hour	Summary of Events and Information	Remarks and references to Appendices
ELVERDINGHE	1915 Sept 25		2nd Phase 4.56 am to 5.30 am	
		9R Battery	Repeat 1st phase 26 rounds shrapnel	
		8R "	ditto 36 " "	
		C/63 "	ditto 100 " "	
		7R "	Sent Esstimonds to Mackensen Farm 40 ro shrapnel	
		11R "	Sentered EOLIAN FARM, MACKENSEN FARM OSCAR FARM and C7r.r.3.	
			Sniper turned on of 9R Battery to seize opportunity to fire on any enemy that appear thereabouts.	
			Enemy replied with 707 shells with about 20 fair shells in B.21.	
			Remainder of the morning quiet.	
			The following telegram was received on the registration at Tintal from H.Q. 49R Divn.	
			"2nd Army forwards following message received from G.H.Q.	

WAR DIARY
or
INTELLIGENCE SUMMARY.
(Erase heading not required.)

Army Form C. 2118.

Place	Date	Hour	Summary of Events and Information	Remarks and references to Appendices
ELVERDINGHE	1915 April 25		"Chief wishes troops to be impressed that to feels confident they will realize how much our success in the forthcoming operations depends upon the individual efforts of each officer in command. Officers and men must the make this to be enjoined to them totally and in such a manner as will also close our intentions to the enemy."	
		7.15 am	All batteries received message to retaliate from 145th Infty Brigade. 7th Battery fired. Tree made at working party at EOLIAN FARM SS. C.2.5. All batteries fired occasional rounds on points known to be during the enemy's operations in order to stop linking wires. Report received that the Artillery fire on the enemy's front line trench was very effective. The parapet being badly damaged. Very little firing from enemy all day. Observation very difficult all day owing to fog and mist.	SS. C.2.5.

WAR DIARY
or
INTELLIGENCE SUMMARY.
(Erase heading not required.)

Army Form C. 2118

Place	Date	Hour	Summary of Events and Information	Remarks and references to Appendices
ELVERDINGHE	1915 Sept 26		All batteries fired on points contained yesterday morning. 8" Battery fired four rounds on Poesen at C6a5?. C/63rd Battery reported own Rounds at C1a7?. BOESINGHE shelled between them at 2pm. by 5.9 guns. Very quiet day. 11pm enemy fired 2 heavy shells on cross roads at C2.c.5?.	
	27		8" Battery fired ne return on PICKEM CROSS C2C5.9. Very quiet all day. C/63 Battery again fire on Brigade opposite E.29 at request of Infantry. All batteries acted upon to retaliate at 9.25 am.	
	28		7" Battery fired 20 rounds on German front line trenches. C/- Battery fired at 14 rounds at shields on trench running N.E. from HOUSE 10. (C76.93). 1/A (How) battery fired on "T" (C7c8.9) and trenches near KIEL COTTAGE (C7d.5.6) at request of infantry.	

WAR DIARY or INTELLIGENCE SUMMARY

Army Form C. 2118

Place	Date	Hour	Summary of Events and Information	Remarks and references to Appendices
ELVERDINGHE	1915 Sept 28		Enemy shelled SKIPTON ROAD C.13.c.5.5. at 3.15 p.m. and 9ᵗʰ Battery position B.16.a.9.3. at 7.50 a.m.	Kent 2F/YW 1/200000
		10.30 a.m	BRIELEN and 9ᵗʰ Battery O.P. at B.12.c.9.9. shelled.	
	29		7ᵗʰ Battery fired salvos on working party at FOTIAN PY. C.9.c.2.5.	
		10 am	(Notts Battery) shelled FLEET STREET (C.19.a.2.0.) Canal Bank C.13.c.5.2. shelled at 1.45 pm.	
		3.45pm	Enemy shelled our Rampart Trenches at C.9.c.4.8. Enemy artillery very active during the afternoon after a period of comparative quiescence which had existed since the bombardment on the 25ᵗʰ.	
			ELVERDINGHE shelled 4.20 pm — 6.30 pm.	
	30		7ᵗʰ Battery fired salvos on working party at PICKEM CROSS Rds. Three rounds at working party at C.2.c.5.4.	C.2C.73.
		9ᶜ	" " " four rounds at working party at C.2.c.7.3. and C.2.c.5.2.	C.2C.73 and C.2C.5.2

Army Form C. 2118.

WAR DIARY
or
INTELLIGENCE SUMMARY.
(Erase heading not required.)

Instructions regarding War Diaries and Intelligence Summaries are contained in F. S. Regs., Part II. and the Staff Manual respectively. Title pages will be prepared in manuscript.

Place	Date	Hour	Summary of Events and Information	Remarks and references to Appendices
ZILLEBEKE	Sept 20		Fire made first by 9th Battery forward from at Seven S. of PICKEM at C9a.6.6.	11th (How) Batty remained in rear.
		2.15pm	Enemy shelled road E. of WHITE HOPE CORNER (No2.75) for half an hour. Very quiet day. Registration of 49th Siege Artillery Zones 3rd W.R. Zone — C13.6.98 to C9a.2.3. Communications — 3rd W.R. F.A. Bde in communication with 2nd W.R. F.A. Bde. Left Inf. Bde Commander Right Group Head Qrs (had not wire from Bde.) All Batteries in communication with one another with Station the O.C. of Infty Bty directly support also with Company Commander in front line trenches.	

1577 Wt. W10791/1773 500,000 1/15 D. D. & L. A.D.S.S./Forms/C. 2118.

49th Division

12/7400

1/3 W.R. Bde R.F.A.

Vol VI

Oct /15

WAR DIARY
October 1915

1/3rd West Riding Brigade R.F.A.T.

WAR DIARY
or
INTELLIGENCE SUMMARY.
(Erase heading not required.)

Army Form C. 2118.

Place	Date	Hour	Summary of Events and Information	Remarks and references to Appendices
ELVERDINGHE	1915 Oct.	1	Hostile aeroplanes active. Quiet day morning. 9th Battery in action at S15 c 7.7 pulled about to observe batteries did not fire.	
		2	Quiet day - batteries did not fire. Enemy fired several minnies in A24b during the morning and infantry fire.	
		3	7th Battery fired one salvo on working party at C9 a 9.2. 9th Battery registered C11 a 9.8 and road to PROVEN. Enemy shelled B10 a 27 with 70 rounds 5.9.	
		4	9th Battery fired 8 rounds on working party at C8 a 5.8 and 6 rounds in registration of C9 a 2 8. 9th Battery fired 11 rounds from forward gun on working party at C8 a 4.2. Aeroplane shelled 11.40 am. Three enemy observation balloons up.	

WAR DIARY or INTELLIGENCE SUMMARY

Army Form C. 2118.

Place	Date	Hour	Summary of Events and Information	Remarks and references to Appendices
ELVERDINGHE	1915 Oct 4		during the day at 26°, 134°, and 60° magnetic from B.22.d.18. Capt. H.R.Vickers of the D.A.C. joined for course of instruction and attached to 7th Battery.	
		2.40 pm	Railway in BOESINGHE heavily shelled.	
		5.34 pm 5.43 pm 5.32 pm	All batteries retaliated at 5.34pm 5.43pm 5.32pm	
	5		Retaliation message rec'd at 6.47 am – all batteries fired one salvo.	
		3.5 pm	7th Battery fired on enemy working party at G.14.a.6.8 and on their office for forward gun and registered it on enemy trench from C.14.a.9.1 to C.14.b.9.3. Registered battery on enemy trench at C.7.a.2.1 to C.7.a.2.3. 8th Battery registered trenches from C.7.a.2.1 to B.12.6.97. 9th Battery registered trenches from B.12.b.6.8 to B.6.d.3.2.	
		4 pm to 4.15 am	Enemy heavily bombarded road running from WHITE HOPE CORNER (B.10.d.5.6.) to BOESINGHE. Three batteries fired but could not be located.	

Army Form C. 2118.

WAR DIARY
or
INTELLIGENCE SUMMARY.
(Erase heading not required.)

Instructions regarding War Diaries and Intelligence Summaries are contained in F.S. Regs., Part II. and the Staff Manual respectively. Title pages will be prepared in manuscript.

Place	Date	Hour	Summary of Events and Information	Remarks and references to Appendices
ELVERDINGHE	1915 Oct 5		He fell orders were issued respecting S.O.S. calls from French on our left. "In the event of an attack on our left (trench area) 9" Battery - Will fire on trenches B1a.6.8 to B6d.3.2 and all Communication trenches leading up to them. 8" Battery - Will fire on trenches B12.6.9.7 & B1a.6.88. and Communication trenches leading thereto, South of the railway. 7" Battery - Will fire on trenches C7a.2.1. to C7.a.2.3. and Communication trenches running N.E. from FARM 14 and due EAST from POINT 23.	Trench map Boesinghe Troens
	6		9" battery fired 4 rounds at a party of 11 Germans seen going up the hill at C8a.7.7. Enemy shelled BOESINGHE with high velocity battery - few salvos of four guns.	

WAR DIARY
or
INTELLIGENCE SUMMARY.

(Erase heading not required.)

Army Form C. 2118.

Place	Date	Hour	Summary of Events and Information	Remarks and references to Appendices
ELVERDINGHE	1915 Oct 7		7th Battery fired salvo on working party at C.14.a.7.7. and one round from forward gun into enemy trench at KRUPP FARM C14.a.91. Very quiet day.	
	8		9th Battery fired five rounds in registration of _____ gun in advance from forward position. Enemy fired about 60 heavy shells into MODDER FARM b.7.a.8.5. Day quiet and very misty.	
	9		BOESINGHE shelled during the afternoon. Quiet day.	
	10		7th Battery fired four rounds from forward gun at enemy Communication trenches at VON KLUCK FARM C14.6.9.4. 9th Battery fired salvo at JOLIE FARM C.9.a.2.8. which is suspected of being an observation station.	

1577 Wt.W10791/1773 500,000 1/15 D. D. & L. A.D.S.S./Forms/C. 2118.

WAR DIARY or INTELLIGENCE SUMMARY

Army Form C. 2118.

Place	Date	Hour	Summary of Events and Information	Remarks and references to Appendices
ELVERDINGHE	1915 Oct 10		9th battery fired three rounds at working party at OSCAR FARM C8a 6.3. Very misty until noon – then heat lifted. Somewhat large German working parties were observed behind trench running N.E. from C8a 6.3.	
	11		All batteries recd orders to establish at 140pm and ready eg 7. Zero hour when held at 3pm will be 3rd will style traversing fire the brigade took 3 first and 2 second prizes. MALAKOFF FARM O.22 d.4.10 shelled and some made to fire heavy 1 shelled BOESINGHE with heavy trench mortars. The Germans apparently have two machine guns at BOESINGHE which they use as anti-aircraft guns.	
		4.15 pm	ELVERDINGHE CHATEAU and grounds shelled by hostile 5.9 battery – 2 guns firing about 30 rounds.	

Army Form C. 2118.

WAR DIARY
or
INTELLIGENCE SUMMARY.

(Erase heading not required.)

Instructions regarding War Diaries and Intelligence Summaries are contained in F. S. Regs., Part II. and the Staff Manual respectively. Title pages will be prepared in manuscript.

Place	Date	Hour	Summary of Events and Information	Remarks and references to Appendices
ELVERDINGHE	1915 Oct. 12		8th Battery fired 13 rounds at trench mortar at B12 b.7.3. at request of 146th Infty Bgde.	Ref Sheet 28 N.W. 2/20000
		1pm	Enemy shelled BOESINGHE with 7.7 cm and 10.5 cm guns. TUGELA FARM shelled at 1.40 pm (B18 b.35.) ELVERDINGHE shelled for half an hour at 5.15 pm.	
	13		7th Battery fired 15 rounds from forward gun (B18 c 54) at trenches running from KRUPP FARM (C14 a 91) to C14 b 93. Enemy retaliated by firing 6 salvos from light field guns into our front line trenches. ELVERDINGHE shelled at 5.15 pm by what was apparently a 4.7 inch gun firing French ammunition. Bearing taken from blind shell 73½° magnetic from B14 d 10.9. Enemy artillery active up to 11 pm.	
	14		All batteries retaliated at 9.50 pm last night (14/15-?). Each battery fired two salvos.	N.L.

WAR DIARY
or
INTELLIGENCE SUMMARY.
(Erase heading not required.)

Army Form C. 2118.

Instructions regarding War Diaries and Intelligence Summaries are contained in F.S. Regs., Part II and the Staff Manual respectively. Title pages will be prepared in manuscript.

Hour, Date, Place	Summary of Events and Information	Remarks and references to Appendices
ELVERDINGHE 1915 OCT 14	Quiet day - very heavy mist all day.	
15	Very quiet day. Heavy mist. All batteries retaliated at 2.27pm. Enemy shelled BOESINGHE CHATEAU during the morning and TALANA FARM (B12 c.9.7.)	
16		
17	Very quiet and misty.	
18	9 K Battery fired four rounds on working parties between C8 a 7.6 and C8 a 6.8. Patrols reported audible all along German trenches from C7c.2.0 to C7 a.2.3 and also along German trench from C7a.v.f to C7 c.n.3 where wire appeared double wide at the top and no blind turn. 8.45pm Enemy shelled BOEDINGHE CHATEAU 9.30pm Enemy put 32 shots about in B15 c 4.3.	LIEUT H.G. HOWSON appointed ADC to MAJGEN PERCIVAL C.B. CBO commanding 49th Divn. BOESINGHE HWD 10/10/15 10 rounds of which 3 are blind.

WAR DIARY
or
INTELLIGENCE SUMMARY.
(Erase heading not required.)

Army Form C. 2118.

Hour, Date, Place	Summary of Events and Information	Remarks and references to Appendices
ELVERDINGHE Oct 1915 19.	All batteries retaliated at 2.25 pm. 7th Battery fired three rounds on working party at advanced trench of infantry. Enemy aeroplanes very active during the morning. 6th Artillery Brigade shelled with 5.9 howitzers and aeroplane observation - 12 rounds 5.9 how. One direct hit on dug out but no casualties. 9th Battery our positon shelled at 2.15 p.m.	
20	7th Battery fired 6 rounds on working party at request of Infantry. 9th Battery 4 rounds on working party on PILCKEM RIDGE CFa.57. BOESINGHE shelled intermittently during the day.	

(73989) W4141—463. 400,000. 9/14. H.&J.Ltd. Forms/C. 2118/10.

WAR DIARY
or
INTELLIGENCE SUMMARY.
(Erase heading not required.)

Army Form C. 2118.

Instructions regarding War Diaries and Intelligence Summaries are contained in F. S. Regs., Part II and the Staff Manual respectively. Title pages will be prepared in manuscript.

Hour, Date, Place	Summary of Events and Information	Remarks and references to Appendices
ELVERDINGHE 1915 Sept 21	7th Battery fired Three salvos on working party at C.8.c.2.6. Very thick mist in the morning. Brigade supplied with 18 pdr guns. 7th Battery attached to Centre Group in redistribution of Groups.	
""	Left Group consisting now of 7th and 8th Batteries with one section of howitzers attacked from 4h.40m Rifle.	
22	8th and 9th Batteries retaliated at 12.9 pm and again at 12.20 pm when two salvos were fired. Canal bank heavily shelled by enemy. One 18 pdr gun placed in position in each battery.	
23	Morning and early afternoon being quiet. Canal bank heavily shelled during afternoon.	

WAR DIARY
or
INTELLIGENCE SUMMARY.
(Erase heading not required.)

Army Form C. 2118.

Hour, Date, Place	Summary of Events and Information	Remarks and references to Appendices
ELVERDINGHE	**1915**	
	Oct 23. ELVERDINGHE heavily shelled during the night 23/24th at 11.20 p.m and 1.5 a.m. Two shells struck Brigade Hd Qrs 5.9 but no casualties. Very heavy wind all day and throughout the night.	
	24. S.A Battery carried out registration of 18 pdrs from 9ᵀᴴ – – – – – –	
	25. Enemy batteries continued registration. Very heavy wind all day.	
	26. Registration continued. 9ᵀᴴ Battery fired on working party at C1 d 9. Enemy fired 2 salvos at CHASSEUR FARM B11 d.2.2. (9ᵀᴴ Battery O.P.) BOESINGHE bombarded with trench mortars and aerial torpedoes.	

Army Form C. 2118.

WAR DIARY
or
INTELLIGENCE SUMMARY.
(Erase heading not required.)

Instructions regarding War Diaries and Intelligence
Summaries are contained in F. S. Regs., Part II.
and the Staff Manual respectively. Title pages
will be prepared in manuscript.

Hour, Date, Place	Summary of Events and Information	Remarks and references to Appendices
ELVERDINGHE 1915 Oct 27.	8th Battery reported 9th Battery fired on working party at C7c79. 8th Battery shelled by 15 cm. battery	
28	Very misty. Enemy shelled CONSEUR FARM 9am	
29	8th & 9th batteries reported Enemy shelled CONSEUR FARM B11 a 2.2.	
30	8th Battery fired on enemy's front line trenches at request of 7th Inf. Regt 8th & 9th Batteries continued registration CONSEUR FARM B11 a 3.2. Enemy shelter and practically destroyed.	
31	9th Battery fired on working party at C7c7.8 and also by request of the French, on B12.b.7.5. 9th battery attacked hire -8 rounds of 10 am, German trench mortars active in front of BOESINGHE.	Lieut G.T. GOODMAN joins the Brigade and posted to 8th Bn. D.C.

(73989) W4141—463. 400,000. 9/14. H.&J.,Ltd Forms/C. 2118/10.

X Corps.
49th Div.

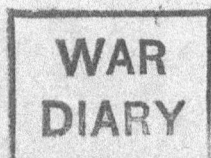

Headquarters,

247th BRIGADE, R.F.A.

J U L Y

1 9 1 6

INTELLIGENCE SUMMARY

(Erase heading not required.)

Place	Date	Hour	Summary of Events and Information	Remarks and references to Appendices
Englebelmer	1/6		"Z" Day. All Divisions carry out tasks allotted in attached Counter Battery Programme.	Reference map held 5Td S.E.
		7.30 a.m.	Infantry launch attack. 32nd and 36th Divisions on the line, 49th and 25th Divisions in reserve.	
		2.25 p.m.	7.0.0 at 0.9.32.L reports that German Infantry and Cavalry can be seen advancing K.20a. Batteries ordered to form barrage.	
		5.45 p.m.	7.0.0 at 9.32 reports that trench no A.20a seems to be held by Germans. The Buhot appears to be holding the trench L.19.R.5.0 to L.20.a.8.5.? and are well massed. The Germans appear to have come over the crest at R.4 to make the counter attack, and made a flanking movement on our troops. They came through the hedge at R.19.b from direction of Beaucourt, and entered intersection of trench at L.14.c.I.I.	[signature]

INTELLIGENCE SUMMARY

(Erase heading not required.)

Place	Date	Hour	Summary of Events and Information	Remarks and references to Appendices
Englebelmer	1/7	5.45 pm	Our troops appeared to be disorganged when they commenced to retire. They halted at the top of the hill in R.1.b. this caused a muddle, the Buthak and German trench getting intermixed, and it looked as though the Germans took a considerable number of our men as prisoners. It was an organised retirement on our part, although at one time it appeared otherwise, and turned out to be a splendid rearguard action.	
		6.15 pm 7.00 at 7.22 pm	starts station shell. seems very doubtful. Germans can be seen laying out the bank at R.19.d.9.8.	
	2/7	11.25am 2.0 pm 3.0pm	A Battery carried out Counter Battery Orders. Gun fired on night lines at 10 rounds an hour for Battery until 2.0 pm Increased rate to 60 rounds an hour until 3.10 pm	

INTELLIGENCE SUMMARY

Instructions regarding War Diaries and Intelligence Summaries are contained in F.S. Regs., Part II and the Staff Manual respectively. Title Pages will be prepared in manuscript.

(Erase heading not required.)

Place	Date	Hour	Summary of Events and Information	Remarks and references to Appendices
Englebemer	2/16		"E" Battery. Carried out Gunners' Battery Orders	
			27 rounds fired on Targets 51	
			29 " " " 48	
			52 " " " 47	
			12 " " " 65	
		5.57pm	169 Rounds fired on A/4 + and d	
		7.20/8	39 rounds fired on A/4c & A 20 t	
		7.40pm	51 Rounds fired on A/4 a	
		10pm to 4.30am	159 Rounds fired on A 7 a & A 8 c	
		11.25am to 3pm	Fired on night lines at rate of 10 rounds per hour	
		3pm to 3.15pm	Fired on night lines at 60 rounds an hour	
			"D" Battery	
		5.10pm	10 rounds fired on A.28.c.90. Counter Battery.	
			10 rounds fired on A.32.b.1.6	

INTELLIGENCE SUMMARY

(Erase heading not required.)

Instructions regarding War Diaries and Intelligence Summaries are contained in F.S. Regs., Part II and the Staff Manual respectively. Title Pages will be prepared in manuscript.

Place	Date	Hour	Summary of Events and Information	Remarks and references to Appendices
Engelbelmer	2/6	6.45 to 7.15 pm	D Bakery. Fired 10 rounds on R.15.c.3.1. Sunken Bakery.	
		6.38 pm	34 rounds on R.14.a.k.b.	
		6.30 to 7.30 pm	30 rounds on R.13.c.5.5. supposed enemy concentration	
		10.15 to 11 pm	159 rounds on R.27.b.5.2. R.28.c.9.0. R.28.c.9.4. R.24.b.1.6. Sunken Bakery.	
			During night 100 rounds fired on Sunken Road and Intermediate trench in R.13.a and R.13.b.3.5.c	
		12.10 pm	20 rounds fired on R.28.c.9.4 to 9.0 Sunken Bakery	
		2.30 pm	20 rounds on R.9.a.5.3.	
	3/6		A. Bakery	
		5 pm	1 Salvo fired on Target 57	
		5.5/6 6.5 pm	60 rounds fired on 67 to 58 Sunken Bakery	
		7.20 pm	20 rounds fired on R.9.d.6.0	
		8.57 pm	20 rounds fired on Target 65.	

INTELLIGENCE SUMMARY

or

(Erase heading not required.)

Instructions regarding War Diaries and Intelligence Summaries are contained in F. S. Regs., Part II. and the Staff Manual respectively. Title Pages will be prepared in manuscript.

Place	Date	Hour	Summary of Events and Information	Remarks and references to Appendices
Engelbelmer	8/10	9.30 pm	A.Bakery. Fire at rate of 15 rounds per hour fired on R.20 d 7.1	
		10.15 pm to 10 am	Fire at intervals on Courcelette Bakery target	
		10.58 pm	1 Schau ordered to fire on Northern Counter Attack	
		11.15 am	Other Schau commenced	
		11.53 am	Ceased fire. 150 rounds fired in all	
		11.15 am	Irregular bursts on Targets 57 and 58 and sweeping up to cross roads in R.15 a 80/60. 10 rounds in all	
		2.25 pm 2.55 pm	84 rounds fired on Targets 67 and 69	
			C.Bakery. Counter Bakery orders carried out C.	
			313 rounds on Target 57 Courcelette Bakery	
			2 " " " 48	
			49 " " " 47	
			75 " " " 65	
			30 " " " 546	
			47 " " " 57	
			" " " 49	

signed

INTELLIGENCE SUMMARY

or

(Erase heading not required.)

Instructions regarding War Diaries and Intelligence Summaries are contained in F. S. Regs., Part II. and the Staff Manual respectively. Title Pages will be prepared in manuscript.

Place	Date	Hour	Summary of Events and Information	Remarks and references to Appendices
Englebelmer	2/10		E Battery	
		6pm	41 rounds fired R.21 d.90/30 to R.15a.	
		1.15pm	20 rounds on Cross Roads R.15a.	
		9.30pm	270 rounds on rifle lines	
		5.30 am	439 rounds on Railway.	
		6.25pm to 9.30pm	60 rounds fired on R.14 & R.20.	
			"D" Battery	
		4.30 to 5.30 pm	78 rounds on R.15 & S.2 with aeroplane observation	
		6pm	29 rounds on R.15 d.01/60. Counter Battery	
		5 to 5.15pm	37 rounds on R.21 a 55/60 aeroplane observation	
		During afternoon	60 rounds on Sunken Road R.14 d. & R.15 c	
		11.45pm	12 Gas Shell in Arrancourt	
		12.30 am	8 " " Arrancourt	
		During night	55 rounds Sunken Road R.14 d. R.15 c & R.15 d. 3.5	
	3rd	5 am	10 rounds R.15 c 3.1 - Counter Battery.	

INTELLIGENCE SUMMARY

(Erase heading not required.)

Instructions regarding War Diaries and Intelligence Summaries are contained in F.S. Regs., Part II. and the Staff Manual respectively. Title Pages will be prepared in manuscript.

Place	Date	Hour	Summary of Events and Information	Remarks and references to Appendices
Enfidaville	3/10	5 a.m.	"J" Battery. 10 rounds R15a 07/60. Counter Battery	
		7 a.m.	157 Ano Shells on R28 = 90 to 94. R34 d 1.6	
		9.45 a.m.	25 rounds on R28c 9.0 – 9.4. Counter Battery R34 d 1.6	
		10.10 a.m.	20 rounds on R21 a 35/90 to R15c 55/30	
		10.25" – 12.25 pm	35 rounds on R29c 50/05 to R35a 60/85 (Aeroplane observation)	
		3.20 to 3.45 pm	32 Incendiary Shells on Grand count. Not very effective	
	4/10		"J" Battery.	
		12.40 a.m.	22 rounds fired on R20a 9.1 to R27a 9.9.	
		12.45 a.m.	52 rounds fired on target 68.	
		3.30 pm	377 rounds fired on Northern Counter Attack	
		3.30 pm	20 rounds fired on target 97 to 59	
		4 pm	22 rounds fired on R26 c	

INTELLIGENCE SUMMARY

(Erase heading not required.)

Place	Date	Hour	Summary of Events and Information	Remarks and references to Appendices
Englebelmer	4/1/16	12.30am	"C" Battery — 6 rounds fired on Railway.	
		3.30pm	87 rounds fired on Northern Counter Attack.	
			"D" Battery	
		12.30 & 1am	12 rounds fired on R18 & R15 and Sunken Road R.H.A. & R15c.	
		10.50pm 16/ 12.30am	50 rounds fired on R13 & and d.	
		11am 16/ 1pm	12 rounds fired on Grandcourt.	
		2.15pm	30 rounds fired on R15 & R.11.15.36. Counter Battery	
		2.25pm	28 rounds fired on Sunken Road R.20 a.	
			"A" Battery	
4th 5th 5/1/16		9.4pm to 3am	108 Rounds fired on Targets 59 & T.	
4/1/16		9.30pm to 6.10am	141 Rounds fired on Working parties R.21c 10/80 & R.27 & 10/80	

INTELLIGENCE SUMMARY

(Erase heading not required.)

Instructions regarding War Diaries and Intelligence Summaries are contained in F.S. Regs., Part II. and the Staff Manual respectively. Title Pages will be prepared in manuscript.

Place	Date	Hour	Summary of Events and Information	Remarks and references to Appendices
Englebmer	4/6	9.40pm to 5.50am	"C" Bakery. 120 rounds fired on Sargos 51 & 246.	
	4/6	9.20pm to 9.30am	84 rounds fired on R 21 d 00/15	
	5/6	1.45pm	12 rounds fired on target 40	
	4/6	8.30pm	"D" Battery. 20 rounds fired on R28 c 9.4 and 9.0. R 34 b.1.6 and 7.7	
		12 md.	Enemy fires on Englebmer Court.	
	5/6	During night 10am	10.9 rounds fired on R 28 c 9.4 + 9.0. R 28 a 7.0 + 6.4 R 34 b.1.6 and 7.7 Camden Battery.	
		9.30am	Sheeks Avenue shelled with 5.9's Thiepval lightly shelled with 77 mm.	
		2.30pm to 3.45pm	Intermittent shelling of Beaune during day. Unknown shelling of Hamel	

INTELLIGENCE SUMMARY

or

(Erase heading not required.)

Place	Date	Hour	Summary of Events and Information	Remarks and references to Appendices
Englebelmer	5/7/16	12noon	Enemy Trenches and Machine Gun have been shelled at intervals with 15 cm. How. and 10.5 cm gun firing from direction of GRANDCOURT.	
		5 to 7 pm	Heavy trenches shelled. Heavy-bombardment and also shelled	
		7.45pm	'E' Battery 50 rounds on R.28.c.9.4/90 and R.28.d.30/60 also R.34.b.1.6 + 1.7 and Grandcourt + R.15.a 32 rounds on Cross Roads	
			'A' Battery 10 rounds fair hour fired during night on targets 47 + 59.	
	6/7/16	6.30am	'C' Battery fired 30 rounds on 3 + 6 + 51.	
		2.30pm	Enemy trenches shelled at intervals	
		10 pm	'D' Battery fired 24 rounds onto Grandcourt	
		11.30pm	'B' Battery fires 20 rounds on R.21.a.5.5/90	
			'A' Battery	
	7/7/16	1.50am	Fired 50 rounds on Targets 59 to 47.	
		1.40am	'C' Battery fired 10 rounds on Targets 51.	
			X Corps attack OVILLERS LA BOISELLE	
		6 am	Infantry launch attack	

INTELLIGENCE SUMMARY

Summaries are contained in F.S. Regs., Part II. and the Staff Manual respectively. Title Pages will be prepared in manuscript.

(Erase heading not required.)

Place	Date	Hour	Summary of Events and Information	Remarks and references to Appendices
Engelbelmer	7/6	8.15 to 8.15 am	"A" Battery fired on target 51. 8.15 to 8.30 am fired one round per gun per 2 minutes on targets 51-63	
		8.30 k		
		8.45 am	Fired one round per gun per minute on 51-63.	
		10.40 am	3 rounds per gun on 51-63	
		11.15 am	30 rounds on targets 51 to 63.	
		2 pm.	24 rounds on targets 51 to 63.	
			C. Battery	
		8.15 am to	115 rounds fired on Target 48.	
		2.15 pm		
		11.40 am to 2.15 pm	23 rounds fired on Target 546	
			D. Battery	
		8.15 am to 2.15 pm	132 rounds fired on R.21 a 55/90 + R.28 c 9.4 + 9.0 also R.34 b.1.6	
		10.10 am to 11 am	25 rounds Incendiary Shell on THIEPVAL CHATEAU R.25 c 25/55.	

INTELLIGENCE SUMMARY
(Erase heading not required.)

Place	Date	Hour	Summary of Events and Information	Remarks and references to Appendices
Englebelmer	7/10	5.51 pm	"A" Battery — Fired 2 salvos on Working Party at R.31.d.30/20 to R.27.a.90/75.	
		6.45 pm	Fired 2 salvos at Working Party at R.27 & 61/39.	
		6.52 pm	Fired 20 rounds on Targets 51 to 63	
		7.40 pm	4 rounds on R.21.d.44/40	
		11.56 pm to 5 am	Fired 30 rounds and kept sweeping 47, 40, 49, 7, 45 and 59.	
	8/10		"C" Battery	
	7/10	5.53 am	2 salvos at Working Party on R.31.d.30/20 to R.27.a.90/75"	
		6.40 pm	8 rounds on R.27 & 61.39	
		11.59 pm to 5 am 8th	150 rounds on 51 and 63	
			"D" Battery —	
		4.30 pm	Fired 4 rounds on Enemy count	
		6 pm	18 rounds on R.2.a. & 3 Working Party — dispersed	
		7.30 pm	11 rounds thus R.29.c.5.0 by aeroplane observation	
	8/10	12 midnight to 5 am	20 rounds fired on R.15 & 3.2 and 19 rounds on R.9.d.5.3	

INTELLIGENCE SUMMARY

(Erase heading not required.)

Instructions regarding War Diaries and Intelligence Summaries are contained in F.S. Regs., Part II. and the Staff Manual respectively. Title Pages will be prepared in manuscript.

Place	Date	Hour	Summary of Events and Information	Remarks and references to Appendices
Engelbelmer	8/10		"D" Battery	
		11.15 am	Fired 6 rounds on Grandcourt.	
		12.30 pm / 1 pm	} 20 rounds on R.28.c.9.0 by aeroplane observation	
		1.10 pm	20 rounds fired on A.28.c.9.0 and 9.4 also R.34.6.16.	
		4.15 / 7.30 pm	81 rounds fired on A.28.c.9.0.6.9.4 + R.32.6.1.6.	
		7.30 pm / 8.30 pm	} 80 rounds fired on A.28.c.9.4. Aeroplane observation	
		During night	71 rounds on R.28.c.9.0.6.9.4 + A.52.6.1.6.	
	9/10	11.10 / 11.40 am	} 36 rounds on — do —	
		11.52 am	6 rounds on A.28.c.9.4.	
		12.30 pm	36 rounds on burden Battery targets as above (—do—)	
		3 pm	6 rounds fired on A.15 & 2.1.	

INTELLIGENCE SUMMARY

(Erase heading not required.)

Summaries regarding War Diaries and Intelligence Summaries are contained in F.S. Regs, Part II. and the Staff Manual respectively. Title Pages will be prepared in manuscript.

Place	Date	Hour	Summary of Events and Information	Remarks and references to Appendices
Engelbelmer	9/16		"A" Battery	
		12.5 pm	20 rounds on Target 48	
		1.15 pm	20 rounds on A27 & 05/85 to 50/15.	
		3.15 pm	12 rounds fired on Target 48	
		4.25 pm	20 rounds fired on Target 48	
		5.0 pm	8 rounds in Collaboration 19 & 8.	
		6 to 6.30 pm	40 rounds fired on Targets 8.	
		10.15 pm	20 rounds on 45 and 49	
			"C" Battery	
		5.30 pm	20 rounds on Target 48.	
		10.15 pm	10 rounds on Target 40	
		10.15 pm to —	10 rounds on Target 49.	
			"D" Battery	
		4 to 5 pm	54 rounds fired on L15c 53/30. aeroplane observation	
		6 to 6.30 pm	30 rounds " . L28 c 9.4 : 9.0 also L3t & I.C.	
	10/16	7 am	10 rounds on L28 c 9.0.	
			20 rounds on R28 c 9.4: 9.0 also R29 & I.C.	

INTELLIGENCE SUMMARY

(Erase heading not required.)

Instructions regarding this form: Summaries are contained in F.S. Regs., Part II. and the Staff Manual respectively. Title Pages will be prepared in manuscript.

Place	Date	Hour	Summary of Events and Information	Remarks and references to Appendices
Englebelmer	10/7	10.45am to 12.20pm	D. Battery. 36 rounds on L18 d 6.9; L7 c 1.1. L8 a 7.7 & L19 c 9.7 Registration	
		3/5 3.30pm	24 rounds on L28 c 9.4; 9.0. & L34 b 1.6.	
			A. Battery.	
		4.30pm	12 rounds fired on Target 48.	
		4.35pm	32 " " " " 48	
		4.55pm	32 " " " " 48	
		5.10pm	" " " " 48	
		9.55pm	96	
			B. Battery.	
		6.25pm	12 rounds fired on Target 48	
			D. Battery.	
		4.25pm to 5.10pm	60 rounds on L28 c 9.4; 9.0 also L34 b 1.6	
		7.50pm	3 rounds in Cakstation in L13 d 56	
		9.20pm	8 rounds fired on L34 b 1.6	
		10pm	6 rounds on L28 a 2.8	
11/7	12.45am		8 rounds on R 9 d 5.3 & 3.5 - Bombers Carrying Party	

INTELLIGENCE SUMMARY
(Erase heading not required.)

Place	Date	Hour	Summary of Events and Information	Remarks and references to Appendices
Englebelmer	1/2/16	4.55am 11.20am 1.pm 3.15 pm	A: Battery 57 rounds on enemy 51 N's and N° 68. 42 rounds on Working Party L3 &5.8. fired 10 rounds on A3 & 5.8. 6 rounds on Target L3 &5.8. Enemy observers to be doing considerable work in second line	
MESNIL	1/2/16	6-8pm	Headquarters became Headquarters of Right Artillery Group of 49th Divisional Artillery. The Group being composed of the following batteries. A/247 (Major Clifford) B/247 (Capt Guest) C/247 (Major Jordan) A/153 (Capt Nicholls) B/153 (Capt Holliday) C/153 (Major Wearter) D/153 (Capt Cullen) On our right is Colonel Mueller in command of Artillery Group and on our Left Colonel Whitty in command of 40th Divisional Artillery.	

INTELLIGENCE SUMMARY

(Erase heading not required.)

Place	Date	Hour	Summary of Events and Information	Remarks and references to Appendices
MESNIL	12/7/16		The 8th Suffolks in Brigade Support of the 147th Infantry Bde the 8th Battalion of the 147th Infantry Bde. Occupies the trenches from Q.36 & 1050 to R.25.d.3 inclusive. In addition to the 8th and 9th Suffolks there is a Labouring Group Covering the Area 147 Infants Bde who are called on when emergencies for is required in any particular part of the line. Two men allotty to all platoons and men for S.O.S. fire – Legend Fire – First Trench – Support of Sniper or Flank Fire issued. The Several Artillery Buses are of present any upon the enemy trenches & wire, & cut any wire opening keep a sharp look-out for breaks in any part of the line to fire occasional rounds at irregular intervals on it all wires & found and during the night of keep all wires & Gun in action trenches under a continuous enfilade fire. 1650 rounds per Gun per day are allotted.	

Place	Date	Hour	Summary of Events and Information	Remarks and references to Appendices
MESNIL	12/7/16		Every morning at 4-0 am and every evening at 8-0 pm the following HATE to take place. 4-0 am to 4-10 am } 8-0 pm to 8-10 pm } Barrage on front line trenches in 4-10 am to 4-15 am } Falling Zone. 8-10 pm to 8-15 pm } M.G. on Support line. 4-15 am to 4-20 am } Return to front line. 8-15 pm to 8-20 pm } Rate of fire 2 rds per gun per minute throughout.	
MESNIL	13/7/16		No special news for the day. Back held intermittently with 10·5 cms & 15 cms howitzers. Kowitzer. Scheme issued in accordance with Sir Arty orders. Enemy trenches from R.19.a.2.0 to R.25 & R.20.60 bombarded from – 0·60 minutes to – 0·10 minutes when all batteries in turn.	
MESNIL	14/7/16		Fire on the enemy front line in this	

INTELLIGENCE SUMMARY

(Erase heading not required.)

Place	Date	Hour	Summary of Events and Information	Remarks and references to Appendices
MESNIL	14/7/16		Artillery Zero. From -0.50 Zero fire is lifted 150 yds and from ZERO & +0.5 the fire returns to front line. Bombardment became in intensity from -0.10 to Zero. We occur news of taking of LONGUEVAL – BAZENTIN-le-GRAND village and wood – BAZENTIN-le-PETIT, partly wood.	
		8·0 am		
		1·35 pm	For 5 minutes an intense bombardment of enemy front line in conjunction with a scheme of the infantry who by means of a few shots from a fired shots of the rifle tried to persuade him that an assault is imminent. Enemy imagines that an assault is imminent. The Right and Left flanks of Lgn* Ferrate* D Coy & Lt. Coy find a Lewis officer for the Infantry Brigade (147) in turn for a period of 4 days, and in addition an officer a draft officer for Battalion H.Q. at "Johnston's" Post. *also	
		8·0 pm	Enemy reported to be running from POZIERES along POZIERES-BAPAUME road in hundreds. A large barrage fire was arranged for along POZIERES and they were all said to have front to take full effect.	

INTELLIGENCE SUMMARY

(Erase heading not required.)

Place	Date	Hour	Summary of Events and Information	Remarks and references to Appendices
MESNIL	15/7/16		Enemy этих in back area seems to have been severely reduced and that there is of it to new partly undertaken by flight Felony Ferns.	
			Flight the regular morning and evening HATE to Crucifix. Yesterday Ferns attended.	
	16/7/16.		The regular HATE which was cancelled is revived to date.	
	17/7/16	3-0pm 9-0pm	Place at 3.30 am in a Situated Matr. Two short bombardments in conjunction with left Subs. at 3-0pm & 9-0pm CRUCIFIX (R19 & 25.20) with Staff at 3-0pm & 9-0pm R43 (R20 & 20.70) R25 & 55.70 to junction of road R25 a 5016.	
	18/7/16	3.0pm	3am Division fired out of line altogether so that ere the 153rd Brigade at Crevent in our Scripts. In Exchange to Set the 40th & 46th Batnes of the 38th Artillery regiment. and on our Day 17 to bombard Batnes of the 3 Battns are only Batnes for defence work. but this Erractich bombardment of enemy trenches about LINE of APPLE TREES R31.6.73.75 SP32 a 13.78 — R31.4.37.98 — R31.4.37.98 — R31.4.005 to R31.4.36.55 Crucifix Conjunction bombardment on THIEPVAL with 3 type.	
	19/7/16	8.0pm 10.30pm	Conjunction bombardment of GRANDCOURT with "Slow Special" by 45th & 46th Battns. — 100 rds per battery.	

INTELLIGENCE SUMMARY

(Erase heading not required.)

Place	Date	Hour	Summary of Events and Information	Remarks and references to Appendices
MESNIL	20/7/16	4.45am	Considerable enemy artillery activity on our trench system which was replied to by our counter battery officers.	
		10.45am	Above repeated except that the rest of the day was comparatively quiet.	
			Report received of enemy field gun in action near THIEPVAL. Between 29th German Reserve Corps – O.Ps manned with special look-out for this gun. By the 8th Bavarian Field Artillery Regiment is taken away from no sector in one of attack and we want to exchange B/241 which march in at 5.30pm sharp.	
	21/7/16		Command of Capt Meachin. Group O.P. is started in which there is a telephone Orderly with a direct line east calling O.P. Ir into Communication between F.O.O.s All my th two O.P. is manned by each battery in turn.	

1875   Wt. W593/826 1,000,000 4/15 J.B.C & A. A.D.S.S./Forms/C. 2118.

INTELLIGENCE SUMMARY

(Erase heading not required.)

Place	Date	Hour	Summary of Events and Information	Remarks and references to Appendices
MESNIL	22/7/16	Early morning	Heavy firing is heard but the cause is never discovered by us. As we got no information from Infantry or F.O.O. ohter than Germans shelling around the Sunken Road.	
		10-0pm	A heavy bombardment was heard which contained many hostile guns — preparation for assault of POZIERES.	
	23/7/16 12.30am		Heavy shelling of our trenches in front of THIEPVAL and the attack with D/247m enemy front line at approx by Infantry.	
		3.30am	Smoke barrage reported by our Infantry about LEIPZIG SALIENT. Ring up Right Group and am told that this is our Infantry's doing.	
			Heavy bombardment still continues. Been hero several shells in vicinity of Group HQ. Heavy firing all day and many vague rumours about POZIERES are heard but nothing apparent.	

INTELLIGENCE SUMMARY

(Erase heading not required.)

Summaries are contained in F.S. Regs., Part II. and the Staff Manual respectively. Title Pages will be prepared in manuscript.

Place	Date	Hour	Summary of Events and Information	Remarks and references to Appendices
MESNIL	24/6		A report was received from the Infantry to effect that Rede had been evacuated and that the Gunners (Gunners) had not taken steps to remove it. On investigation by Major Stracen & Capt in conjunction with Bryans Major 141 Infantry this report was found to be false. The Infantry line was stated 1 Qa 3 yards infront the Granatzy Road bups all line open ac again [?]. Distinct orders to keep all line open ac again [?]. Some 10.5 cms Howitzer shells and 10 cms gun shells are again fired at Headquarters. At 10-30 pm a 5 minutes intense bombardment of enemy front line in Battery Zone is carried out from our from Bryans Mgn.	

INTELLIGENCE SUMMARY

(Erase heading not required.)

Place	Date	Hour	Summary of Events and Information	Remarks and references to Appendices
MESNIL	26/7	2.10 am	Left Camp reported an S.O.S. but this was found to be incorrect. A barrage was kept up afterwards until it was definitely reported to be incorrect. There was considerable shelling of our trenches during the morning & this we replied. During the afternoon until about 3.30 pm when a lot then apparently started and our trenches were shelled with all types of projectiles. Whilst our position was also taken in with 15 mm - 10.5 cm Howitzer gun fire and 77 mm field guns - all types of shell were used. 10 cm guns and Howitzers at our Headquarters at the same. Rounds received and Hayonne at our Headquarters at the time, and left with the Colonel for me & our S.P. shot 15 cm made direct hits on an dugouts. Comparatively quiet until 10-30 pm when the enemy fired a stream of tea shell into our vicinity for one hy. an hour. This was and air chief rifts of the same - the air burys shrapnel and trail. With new type ffo shell at rate of about 10 rounds per minute.	[signature]
		10.45		

INTELLIGENCE SUMMARY

(Erase heading not required.)

Summaries are contained in F.S. Regs., Part I. and the Staff Manual respectively. Title Pages will be prepared in manuscript.

Place	Date	Hour	Summary of Events and Information	Remarks and references to Appendices
MESNIL	26/7/16	4:30am	Enemy ceased fire with the gas shell after heavy hget in area of Entonnoirs at 5.3/4 hours during which time he fired between 3 and 4 thousand rounds. In the trenches from there were 12 men killed the rest were stood by two teams stationed on flanes without any casualties on the other men some helmets but all our guns unaffected so far. Clarke, Asst, Orderly Officer, Interpreter & Orderlies are helmets during the gas bombardment and one suspects except for the eyes and a most abominable smell. The only two known cases of men not putting helmets on a firing in a gas fight were done to the neighbouring 1/240 Battery and both died before 10-0 am. Morning very quiet. Heavy cannonade South but nothing of interest. Even Fort de la Hat ridge of POZIERES is down on hand. Joyce sitting on Headquarters at night but nothing of interest. 1875 W. W30/326 1,00,000 4/15 J.B.G & A. A.D.S.S/Form/C/2113. No.J.EROZ16 SALIENT to prevent being seen/becomes approached at night.	
	27/7/16			

INTELLIGENCE SUMMARY

(Erase heading not required.)

Place	Date	Hour	Summary of Events and Information	Remarks and references to Appendices
MESNIL	28/7/16		Nothing of interest.	
	29/7/16		Colonel returns from Wagon Lines after 48 hrs off. Enemy shells fell round Headquarters with 15cm & 21cm howitzers and 15cm gun. Apparently searching and sweeping for 6" (Mark VII) gun fired by MESNIL CEMETERY.	
	30/7/16	10.0pm	Heavy firing in area of BAZIENTIN. Far about from 9.0pm to 10.0pm. Very hot weather. Nothing of interest. Very hot weather.	
	31/7/16		Nothing of interest. Very hot weather.	

signed Arthur Lambert

49th Divisional Artillery.

247th(W.R.) BRIGADE

ROYAL FIELD ARTILLERY.

AUGUST 1 9 1 6

WAR DIARY
or
INTELLIGENCE SUMMARY

(Erase heading not required.)

Place	Date	Hour	Summary of Events and Information	Remarks and references to Appendices
MESNIL	1/8/16	11.30 am	Very hot day. Our lines bombarded by H.A.	
		7.30 pm	Our lines bombarded by H.A.	
			Craters by Tiepval are now almost all in our and others mans employed I secure the enemy.	
	2/8/16		New Blocking Barrage of THIEPVAL and LEIPZIG SALIENT. D. 18-pr. Batteries employed others firing nightly trench, i.e. occasional bursts in Support, Communication and reserve trenches to extent of 100 rounds per battery. Hours of firing are from 10-0 pm to 4-0 am.	
			Received orders that we are to be relieved on 8th inst and Capt. Kitchen Capt R. pk. 248 Bde is ordered to join us so Zone.	

INTELLIGENCE SUMMARY

(Erase heading not required.)

Instructions regarding War Diaries and Intelligence Summaries are contained in F.S. Regs., Part II. and the Staff Manual respectively. Title Pages will be prepared in manuscript.

Place	Date	Hour	Summary of Events and Information	Remarks and references to Appendices
MESNIL	3/8/16		Very hot day.	
		9-30 am	Enemy shelled MESNIL – AUCHONVILLERS road with 5.9 howitzer for about 2 hrs.	
			It is decided to kill or capture all members of a German working party who have been digging a trench N/o Sunken Road in Q.24.d (Sheet 57 D S.E.) at the same time as it have been affirmed a trench south of this road. We are to form a barrage on enemy front line in R.31.c. and support line in R.31.a. and R.31.c. and their did not know come off.	
		11-30 pm	A rapid retaliation on enemy front line in R.31.a. was carried out by all batteries.	
	4/8/16		Hot muggy day. Constant sunshine.	
	5/8/16		Hot day. Comparatively quiet.	
	6/8/16		Hot day. Heard that there is a stunts attack on ANZACS at POZIERES in evening. Dean killed at Group H.Q.	

INTELLIGENCE SUMMARY

(Erase heading not required.)

Place	Date	Hour	Summary of Events and Information	Remarks and references to Appendices
MESNIL	6/6/16		From 7.45 pm until 10.15 pm - a regular shuffle of the country side south of all Aisne including Thiepval. No danger done. Thiepval junction but D/247, Sap Sellin. Annex B/247 keen and Kits a Thur day out and C/247 an freed to clear the telints.	
	7/8/16		Run re finding new Gun positions for an attack on Ovillery front line Ms S of Ancre. Reconnaissance made and position studied.	
	8/6/16	5.30pm	Colonel Stephenson OC 2/8 (H.R.) F.A. Bde takes Command of Centre Group and is return to VARENNES to billets for a Rest.	
VARENNES	9/6/16		Rest day.	
	10/6/16		Rest day with Heavy Showers. Inspection of Clothing etc.	

WAR DIARY
or
INTELLIGENCE SUMMARY
(Erase heading not required.)

Place	Date	Hour	Summary of Events and Information	Remarks and references to Appendices
VARENNES	11/8/16		Inspection of A/247 and D/247 batteries by Colonel.	
	12/8/16		Very hot day. Nothing of interest.	
	13/8/16		Colonel and Adjutant see CRA with view to finding a new emp. Colonel being indisposed Adjutant & Orderly Officer reconnoitre positions for new emp that is to be run as Eighteen emp. Position	
	14/8/16		air. Selected in Q16 a & c. Fine weather breaks up and there is a heavy storm.	
	15/8/16		Nothing of interest.	
	16/8/16		Working party from 20th Durmead. Tunnel Motors is started on new position for new emp. CRA. visits the site.	S.H.
	17/8/16		Work on new position at site of new emp position to proceed with linen Adjutant	

Instructions regarding War Diaries and Intelligence Summaries are contained in F.S. Regs., Part II. and the Staff Manual respectively. Title Pages will be prepared in manuscript.

INTELLIGENCE SUMMARY
or
(Erase heading not required.)

Place	Date	Hour	Summary of Events and Information	Remarks and references to Appendices
VARENNES	18/8/16		Nothing of interest	
	19/8/16		"	
	20/8/16		"	
	21/8/16		"	
	22/8/16		"	
	23/8/16		"	
	24/8/16		Colonel goes to Conference at CRA's office with reference to the proposed attack on the Enemy & the use of live ANGRE.	
	25/8/16		Colonel & Adjutant reconnoitre OPs for wire cutting immediately South of PIERRE Division.	
		5.45pm to 7.45pm	Enemy counter attack in reputed on HOHENZOLLERN REDOUBT. Listening for heavy	JR
	26/8/16		Infantry working party of 40 men to assist 57.TT. men to work on our Artillery position in B.16a.	

1875 Wt. W593/826 1,000,000 4/15 J.B.C. & A. A.D.S.S./Forms/C. 2118.

Place	Date	Hour	Summary of Events and Information	Remarks and references to Appendices
VARENNES	27/8/16		I/c received that the following Batteries will form the ENFILADE GROUP at present being formed:— A/242, A/248, B/243, C/243 — 4 Guns, 4 Guns, 6 Guns, 6 Guns — Commanded by Capt Haynes, " Capt Taylor, " Capt J.D.P Valency, " Major Constantini. The Battery Commanders arrived and were shown round the Battery Positions and O.P.'s and chosen to the 16th Pinned Trench. There is excellent views in enfilade to flanks of the Objective (i.e. Enemy Front Support & Reserve Lines Between Q.24.b.22 and R.25 & 27 & Sheet 57DSE FRANCE 1/20000) During 6th day.	
Q.22.C.10.20. 28/8/16 (34.1.57D.SE) 1/20000			Group Headquarters move into dug-outs at Q.22.C.10.20 and establish communication by means of buried cable with G.H.Q — Centre & left Group — and the four Batteries of the group in Q.16.a & c.	

INTELLIGENCE SUMMARY

(Erase heading not required.)

Instructions regarding War Diaries and Intelligence Summaries are contained in F.S. Regs., Part II and the Staff Manual respectively. Title Pages will be prepared in manuscript.

Place	Date	Hour	Summary of Events and Information	Remarks and references to Appendices
Q22.c.10.20 (FRANCE 57D SE 1/20000)	29/16/8	4-30 am	Batteries are in action and very threatening their emplacements and settling down to the most awful rain when Germans Flugtint the day. Stopped the shooting - Registration impossible. Enemy Aeroplane continually soaring over the battery positions and making a mental note of all their doings without any interference. Owing to the perpetually bad weather the search of the army troubles which should have taken place today is postponed 24 hours. Batteries did anyhow shot when two rounds in their guns. Assault guns destroyed in 24 hours. Batteries re-registered. Battery Zone A/242 Q24.c.11 to Q24.d.55.75 B24.d.50.25 to Q24.d.60.10 and Q24.d.26 to Q24 to 62 R19.c.91 to R25.c.29	[signature]
	30/8/16			
	31/8/16			

1875 Wt. W593/826 1,000,000 4/15 J.B.C. & A. A.D.S.S./Forms/C. 2118.

INTELLIGENCE SUMMARY

(Erase heading not required.)

Place	Date	Hour	Summary of Events and Information	Remarks and references to Appendices
Q.22.c.10.20 (FRANCE 57 SE) (1/20000)	31/8		Battery Zone (Continued)	
		C/243	Q.24 d.5375 to R.19 c.0562	
			Q.24 d.8010 to R.19 c.3080	
			R.19 a.29 to 4.5 to 6.5	
		A/248	R.19 c.0068 to R.19 c.4550	
			R.19 c.3080 to R.19 c.7065	
			R.25 t.29 to R.25 t.36	
		A/243	R.19 c.4065 to R.19 c.9020	
			R.19 c.7065 to R.19 d.0035	
			R.19 d.13 to R.25 H.47	

49th Division

2nd W. R. A. Bde R.F.A.
W. Riding Bd. R.F.A.

War Diary for November 1915

Vol VII

WAR DIARY or INTELLIGENCE SUMMARY

Army Form C. 2118.

(Erase heading not required.)

Hour, Date, Place	Summary of Events and Information	Remarks and references to Appendices
ELVERDINGHE 1915 Nov 1	9" Battery fired on working party at C.7.07.8. and at B.12.6.75 in response to call from the trench on our left. 9" Battery fired also a Trench mortar located nr B.12.6.75 at request of the trench and apparently silenced it. En recurrence Retaliation salvos were fired at enemy's trenches until hostile fire on our front line at F.32 ceased. Continued registration of enemy's strong points and front line trenches. German lined mortars busy in front of BOESINGHE during the afternoon.	LIEUT C. WARDLOW proceeded to hospital sick. Expected and posted to 9" Battery.
2.	Batteries fired in retaliation four times during the afternoon. Enemy shelled BOESINGHE via Trench bridges and S.G.A.	

WAR DIARY
or
INTELLIGENCE SUMMARY.

(Erase heading not required.)

Army Form C. 2118.

Instructions regarding War Diaries and Intelligence Summaries are contained in F.S. Regs., Part II. and the Staff Manual respectively. Title pages will be prepared in manuscript.

Hour, Date, Place	Summary of Events and Information	Remarks and references to Appendices
ELVERDINGHE		
May 1915		
3	9ᵗʰ Battery fired on 012.b.75 (Trench Mortar) at request of the French. Enemy shelled BOESINGHE during the afternoon and ELVERDINGHE at Brigade 4.40 p.m. from apparently the same battery.	
4	5ᵗʰ Battery and 9ᵗʰ Battery continue registration	
5	Batteries received three messages to retaliate from Infty Brigade as enemy was shelling our trenches. BOESINGHE shelled by heavy howitzer battery – 21 rounds of which 12 were blind.	
6	Ordered to fire reserved rounds on enemy Strong points during day & night until evening of 8/9/5 inclusive. ELVERDINGHE shelled at 12.25 p.m. – 6 o'c.r. batteries retaliated on German front line trenches. 9ᵗʰ Battery continued registration.	56 rounds her shrapnel and H.E.

Army Form C. 2118.

WAR DIARY
or
INTELLIGENCE SUMMARY.
(Erase heading not required.)

Instructions regarding War Diaries and Intelligence Summaries are contained in F.S. Regs., Part II. and the Staff Manual respectively. Title pages will be prepared in manuscript.

Hour, Date, Place	Summary of Events and Information	Remarks and references to Appendices
ELVERDINGHE 1918 Nov. 7	Batteries fired four times in retaliation during the day and the enemy received rounds at the rate of 1 per hour on various points in enemy's reserve trenches. ELVERDINGHE shelled at 9.20 am apparently in retaliation for the firing from here. 46 rounds were fired 9 of which were behind and there were apparently 2 or perhaps 3 batteries firing 5.9" and 77 mm. Two duds hits on gun Battery from here. ELVERDINGHE too again shelled at 2.15 pm from same direction - 10 rounds. Weather too misty for observation.	
8.	Both batteries fired occasional rounds during the past 24 hours. Enemy fired about 40 heavier rounds into gun Battery O.P at B12 c 9.9 about 2.5%. There were blind. Registration of enemy's trenches continued.	

WAR DIARY
or
INTELLIGENCE SUMMARY.

(Erase heading not required.)

Army Form C. 2118.

Hour, Date, Place	Summary of Events and Information	Remarks and references to Appendices
ELVERDINGHE 1915 Nov 9	Batteries continued firing on registered points on enemy strong points & retaliation barrage received at 2.40am from enemy. Large working party dispersed by Infantry. BOESINGHE shelled heavily during the morning with field mortars and heavy howitzers. ELVERDINGHE shelled at 12.30pm - 9R Battery retaliated on enemy battery position at C.6.7c.1. Intermittent shelling ensued.	
10	Enemy artillery very active CHASSEUR FARM B11 a 3.2. The 9R Battery O.P was shelled twice during the day. The first time 50 shells were fired at it, 20 of which were blinds. Enemy shelled 60 pdr position at B15 C.6.5 during the afternoon with very accurate fire. Batteries retaliated on enemy trenches and on battery position at C.6.8.4 with H.E. and Shrapnel.	

WAR DIARY or INTELLIGENCE SUMMARY

Army Form C. 2118.

Hour, Date, Place	Summary of Events and Information	Remarks and references to Appendices
ELVERDINGHE 1915 Nov 11	Message received from H.Q.R.A. that information had been received that the enemy intended attack on the YSER on the 11th but no attack took place. Battery continued firing several rounds on 9" Battery fire on a working party in communication trenches at C9.a.5.7, and fire by aeroplane observation at a battery position at C9.b.7½.1. fire on LOMME HOUSE C9.b.2.8 at various infantry targets. The Dutch & German heavily bombarded each others trenches in front of BOESINGHE during the afternoon.	
12	2½" Battery fired on trench mortar reported at C9.a.25. also the remnant of the trench infantry. 9" Battery also fired at the trench mortar. Heavy trench mortar fire in front of BOESINGHE. Battalion retaliated three times during the day in message received from F.O.O.	

(73989) W4141—463. 400,000. 9/14. H.&J.Ltd. Forms/C. 2118/10.

WAR DIARY
or
INTELLIGENCE SUMMARY.
(Erase heading not required.)

Army Form C. 2118.

Hour, Date, Place	Summary of Events and Information	Remarks and references to Appendices
ELVERDINGHE	1915 Nov. 13	Occasional rounds fired by both batteries throughout the day & night ELVERDINGHE shelled at 9.20 p.m. -12 rounds	Ref. Sheet 28 N.W. 1/20000
	14	In conjunction with the heavy artillery the 2nd & 9th Batteries fired on the hostile battery positions at 7.w. am firing 10 rounds HE + 10 minutes from 6 shrapnel each. Every interested in ELVERDINGHE all repeated the operation at 8.15 am	C.1.6.d.1. & U.26.d.4.0.
	15	Received orders to cooperate with the heavy artillery as per operation orders attached. Zero ordered for 6.30 p.m. Very little retaliation by enemy. C/Z & T Batteries fired occasional rounds at fixed points behind the enemy's line during the day	
	16	Band was hand playing apparently near PICKEM 9th battery fired 6 rounds into PICKEM and the band ceased.	

WAR DIARY or INTELLIGENCE SUMMARY

Army Form C. 2118.

Hour, Date, Place	Summary of Events and Information	Remarks and references to Appendices
ELVERDINGHE 1915 Nov 17	Both batteries fired in retaliation at 3.20 a.m. At 3 p.m. a very cloud of fumes vapour was observed in the trenches in front of BOESINGHE. The fire was noticed quite distinctly from one of the observation posts but the infantry apparently was not affected. 5th and 9th Batteries fired a barrage on the trench and went on impeding a working party digging trenches at C.17.2 was fired on and dispersed. Later that an attack was not impending.	
18	Both Batteries fired at report of 5th Batt. W. Riding Regt. Three times during the day and twice at request of the Belch at a Trench Mortar opposite was carried out with a new 6 Howitzer upon a dam in the German trench at B.12 & 10.2 and heavily plastering their line also; however the whole of the work was not effected; our field guns not being heavy enough	

Army Form C. 2118.

WAR DIARY
or
INTELLIGENCE SUMMARY.
(Erase heading not required.)

Instructions regarding War Diaries and Intelligence Summaries are contained in F.S. Regs., Part II. and the Staff Manual respectively. Title pages will be prepared in manuscript.

Hour, Date, Place	Summary of Events and Information	Remarks and references to Appendices
ELVERDINGHE. Nov. 19/15	Two enemy patrols dispersed by S.A. Battery. 9th Battery fired at enemy infantry in B6d & 9z in retaliation for the shelling of Bridge 6.D.	
20	Both batteries fired in retaliation on enemy's front line trench.	
21	Operations were carried out at 10 am in conjunction with the Heavy Artillery. A barrage was also running N.E. from C7a.8.8 in which the numerous dug outs occupied by enemy trench mortar detachments. The fire was very effective, many direct hits being observed, but no movement on the part of the enemy was seen.	Ref. 28 N.W. Sheet 2. 1/10,000
22	Both batteries fired occasional rounds. A very misty day — observation impossible. Men fast.	

WAR DIARY
or
INTELLIGENCE SUMMARY.
(Erase heading not required.)

Army Form C. 2118.

Instructions regarding War Diaries and Intelligence Summaries are contained in F.S. Regs., Part II. and the Staff Manual respectively. Title pages will be prepared in manuscript.

Hour, Date, Place	Summary of Events and Information	Remarks and references to Appendices
ELVERDINGHE 1915 Nov. 23	6th and 9th Batteries registered several points on enemy's trenches.	
24	8th Battery continued registration with gun in new position — one of this gun pits being flooded which made a change of position necessary. 9th Battery fired on trench mortar position at C.10.41 in cooperation with the heavy artillery. ELVERDINGHE shelled during the morning by 5.9" and 4.2" howitzers.	
25	8th Battery shelled a working party at C9a 5.8. This in a trench mortar at C9a 2.3 at the request of the Infantry. Both batteries retaliated on enemy's trenches in response to a message from 107th Inf. Bde. Rec'd information from G.H.Q. that an attack in Flanders (by the enemy this month) was expected during which it was believed a new gas might be used.	

Army Form C. 2118.

WAR DIARY
or
INTELLIGENCE SUMMARY.
(Erase heading not required.)

Hour, Date, Place	Summary of Events and Information	Remarks and references to Appendices
ELVERDINGHE 19/15 Nov. 26	S.P. Battery dropped a German working party seen at C.8.a.5.8. Fired on Trench Mortar at C.7.a.2.3. which had been annoying the French on our left. In the morning the sound of an enemy gun be head of gun behind PILCKEM RIDGE. At the same time a gun was firing from what the same direction thought to be a high muzzle velocity gun firing from range of about 150 m.m. calibre mounted in an armoured train. 27 S.P. Battery fired on supposed machine gun position at C.7.a.5.3 by request of Infty. First time in retaliation during the afternoon for the shelling of our trenches. 9ᵗʰ Artillery came no S.R.	

WAR DIARY or INTELLIGENCE SUMMARY

Army Form C. 2118.

ELVERDINGHE

Hour, Date, Place	Summary of Events and Information	Remarks and references to Appendices
1915 Nov. 28	9th and 7th Batteries fired on machine gun at C.9.a.5.3 at request of infantry.	LIEUT S.J. BLAKE 2LIEUT A.L. HOLMES 2LIEUT D. HURST joined the Brigade and were respectively to Am. Col (not Co) and 9th Bty resp.
	ELVERDINGHE shelled twice during the afternoon. 9th Battery fired on C.2.c.7.3 and C.2.c.5.7 and C.2.c.8.8 in retaliation.	
29	7th Battery fired on the machine gun at C.9.a.5.3 at request of infantry. Enemy working party observed at S.6.6.5.4. Apparently erecting a screen. The party was engaged by a salvo from the 9th Battery but about 20 minutes later the men by a screen were seen to hurt in the middle of the party.	
30	Batteries retaliated twice on enemy trenches at request of infantry. 9th Battery again fired on machine gun at C.9.a.5.3	

S E C R E T.

C.R.A.

1. An Artillery Operation will probably be undertaken by the guns of the 49th Division this afternoon, in co-operation with those of neighbouring formations.

2. The decision as to whether the operation is to take place or not will only be made shortly before it is due to begin. Should the operation take place, retaliation may be expected. The following precautions will, therefore, be taken without further warning.

(i) From 5.p.m. to 8.p.m. troops and transport will be kept away from roads habitually used between those hours and which are exposed to the fire of hostile artillery.

(ii) Troops not on duty, billeted within the commonly shelled area, will be kept under cover from 5.p.m. for the remainder of the night.

                              (sd) A. M. HENLEY, Lt. Colonel.
                     General Staff, 49th (W.R.) Division.
Advd H.Q.
15/11/1915.

-------- 2 --------

To,
    Officers Commanding Batteries.

Forwarded for your information.

                        Captain R.F.A.
                          Adjutant,
             1/3rd West Riding Bde R.F.A.(T).
15/11/1915.

SECRET.

Officer Commanding,
    3rd W.R.F.A.Bdre.

1. Herewith time Table for special operations which will probably be carried out this afternoon.
All arrangements will be made to be ready at a moments notice.

2. Battery Commanders will have their orders ready written for each task, so that each task is carried out to time. The whole success of these operations depends on their being carried out at the time stated.

3. All Batteries will check registration today (this morning) on the enemy's wire and front parapet in their own zone. 12 rounds per battery is allotted for this task.

4. For special Operations, Batteries will come under the Command of their own Brigade Commanders.

     (sd) L. W. LEWER, Major.R.A.
   B.M.R.A. 49th (W.R.) Division.

15/11/1915.

----- 2 -----

To,
  Officers Commanding Batteries,

   The above is forwarded for compliance, please.

        Captain R.F.A.
      Adjutant
  1/3rd West Riding Brigade R.F.A.(T).

15/11/1915.

S E C R E T.   Reference BOESINGHE 1/10,000 Trench Map.

TIME TABLE OF TASKS.

Battery.	Time.	Objective.	Ammunition allotted.
7th BATTERY.	0.p.m.	C 8 a 8.5½	One salvo per Battery (shrapnel)
-do-	20 secs after above.	Approach to OSCAR FARM from PILCKEM ROAD.	-do-
-do-	0.5.p.m.	C 1 d 1.3	-do-
-do-	0.10.p.m.	C 1 d 1.3	-do-
-do-	0.15.p.m.	C 7 a 2.3	-do-
-do-	0.17.p.m.	C 7 b 1.1	-do-
-do-,	0.20.p.m.	C 2 c 8.8	-do-
-do-	0.22.p.m.	C 1 d 10.5	-do-
-do-	0.25.p.m.	C 8 a 8.5½	-do-
8th BATTERY.	0.p.m.	C 8 a 8.9	One salvo of Shrapnel.
-do-	0.5.p.m.	C 1 c 7.1	-do-
-do-	0.10.p.m.	C 1 d. 5.5	-do-
-do-	0.15.p.m.	C 7 a 0.8	-do-
-do-	0.17.p.m.	C 7 a 10.5	-do-
-do-	0.20.p.m.	C 2 c 5.7	-do-
-do-	0.22.p.m.	C 1 d 5.5	-do-
-do-	0.25.p.m.	C 8 a 8.9	-do-
9th BATTERY.	0. 0.p.m.	C 2 c 8.2½	-do-
-do-	0.5.p.m.	C 7 a.1.8	-do-
-do-	0.10.p.m.	C 2 c 3.6	-do-
-do-	0.15.p.m.	C 7 a 2½.2	-do-
-do-	0.17.p.m.	C 1 c 7.1	-do-
-do-	0.20.p.m.	C 2 c 1.5	-do-
-do-	0.22.p.m.	C 1 c 7.1	-do-
-do-	0.25.p.m.	C 2 c 8.2½	-do-

N.B. WATCHES WILL BE CHECKED AT 4.30.p.m.

ZERO will be wired as soon as received from 49th DIV.ARTY. Headquarters, probably about 4.30.p.m.

1/8th West. Ind. Bde. RFA.

War Diary ~ December 1915.

Vol VIII

49 (W.R.) Division

DEC.1995, P1 MISSING

✓ WHEN MARKING UP DOCUMENTS FOR COPYING PLEASE TICK THE APPROPRIATE BOX ON THE OPPOSITE SIDE OF THIS MARKER. THIS INFORMATION IS ESSENTIAL TO ALLOW US TO PROVIDE YOU WITH THE COPIES YOU REQUIRE INFORMATION SHEETS ARE AVAILABLE FROM THE RECORD COPYING COUNTER SHOULD YOU NEED FURTHER ASSISTANCE. *******************************

WAR DIARY or INTELLIGENCE SUMMARY

Army Form C. 2118.

Place	Hour, Date	Summary of Events and Information	Remarks and references to Appendices
ELVERDINGHE	Dec. 7 1915	German aeroplane flying low appeared over the R battery position at 10 a.m. and immediately started to register. Shortly afterwards upwards of 90 shells were fired into the position. As the men had been withdrawn when the registration was over there were no casualties. None of the guns was touched. German artillery was very active all day. ELVERDINGHE was shelled heavily at midday. Each battery fired 60 rounds in retaliation on C8a4.3 and C1a8.0. - hostile battery positions. German aeroplane returned when shelling was over - evidently to observe the result.	
	8	Bombardment of the HIGH COMMAND REDOUBT was reported at 4.45 a.m. by the heavy artillery. The firing was kept up for half an hour. At 6.45 a.m. the enemy retaliated on our trenches and batteries. At 10.30 a.m. to 1.45 p.m. the	

Army Form C. 2118.

WAR DIARY
or
INTELLIGENCE SUMMARY.
(Erase heading not required.)

Hour, Date, Place	Summary of Events and Information	Remarks and references to Appendices
ELVERDINGHE Dec. 8 1915	2ⁿᵈ Battery's position was heavily shelled by at least three batteries. One 200 rounds were fired. The guns were not hit although the position was raked with shells. One man was wounded. Most of the shells fired were 5.9 H.E.	
	9ᵗʰ Battery was called on eight times during the day for retaliation and the 9ᵗʰ Battery fired both batteries engaged hostile batteries at C7a0.6 and U26.C2.8 firing 30 rounds each	
9	9ᵗʰ Battery silenced an enemy machine gun at C7a5.3 at request of infantry. 9ᵗʰ fired 30 rounds together 49 rounds shrapnel on C7c6.8 and C7c7.8 in retaliation for trench mortaring of our trenches.	
10	Operations nil – our high wind all day	

(73989) W4141—463. 400,000. 9/14. H.&J.Ltd. Forms/C. 2118/10.

Army Form C. 2118.

WAR DIARY
or
INTELLIGENCE SUMMARY.
(Erase heading not required.)

Instructions regarding War Diaries and Intelligence Summaries are contained in F. S. Regs., Part II. and the Staff Manual respectively. Title pages will be prepared in manuscript.

Hour, Date, Place	Summary of Events and Information	Remarks and references to Appendices
ELVERDINGHE DEC. 11. 1915	Enemy shelled the ELVERDINGHE – BRIELEN road at ½ hour intervals from 3 am to 7 am – mostly light shrapnel. About 100 rounds were fired round ELVERDINGHE above.	
12	9th Battery dispersed a working party at C.d.9.2. and fired 36 rounds at a sniper's post at C.14 a.1.9½ which had been found. Transit to the hospital. ELVERDINGHE shelled in the afternoon.	
13.	Both batteries fired on working party seen at C.8 a.S.S. and dispersed them. 9th Battery fired 31 rounds into ARTILLERY WOOD C/C 2.3½ by order of Brigade Major R.A. German troops have been seen by the French.	

(73989) W 4141—463. 400,000. 9/14. H.&J.Ltd. Fo-ms/C. 2118/10.

WAR DIARY
or
INTELLIGENCE SUMMARY.
(Erase heading not required.)

Army Form C. 2118.

Instructions regarding War Diaries and Intelligence Summaries are contained in F.S. Regs., Part II. and the Staff Manual respectively. Title pages will be prepared in manuscript.

Hour, Date, Place	Summary of Events and Information	Remarks and references to Appendices
ELVERDINGHE 1915 DEC 14.	8th Battery registered C2 & 43 by aeroplane observation. ELVERDINGHE was shelled in the afternoon about 17 rounds.	
15	8th Battery were called upon to retaliate for times in the evening as the enemy were shelling our trenches. 9th Battery also fired at request of Infantry and fired until it was reported that hostile shelling had ceased.	
16	Very misty all day. Enemy shelled ELVERDINGHE and surroundings for half an hour in the morning - about 50 rounds. 8th Battery fired five times in retaliation.	
17.	8th Battery fired on hostile battery at C.6.c.5.3. - 30 rounds HE & Shrapnel mixed. 9th Battery fired on hostile guns at four	

WAR DIARY
or
INTELLIGENCE SUMMARY.
(Erase heading not required.)

Hour, Date, Place	Summary of Events and Information	Remarks and references to Appendices
ELVERDINGHE Dec. 17. 1915	Support positions C1 & Pt 9. C2 & Pt 1. C.6.9.4 and C.6.10.4. — 20 rounds on each target. 12 noon the bombardment of the enemy's trenches according to operation orders attached. Crumps each 10 had been employed for 2 hours owing to heavy mist.	
Dec 18	Very misty day and consequently quiet to Brigade Artillery 18 rounds. Retaliation at request of Infantry. Fired into the arty firing done by us all day.	
Dec 19th	The days situation opened with 143 rounds shrapnel & 111 rounds H.E. from the 8" & 9.199 rounds shrapnel and 81 rounds H.E. from the 9" Fired on enemy a barrage on the Centre Sectn on account of a S.O.S. from Infantry at 5-30 P.M. The barrage was kept up until 7-30 P.M. when the all was normal except for odd bursts of artillery fire.	

WAR DIARY
or
INTELLIGENCE SUMMARY.
(Erase heading not required.)

Army Form C. 2118.

Hour, Date, Place	Summary of Events and Information	Remarks and references to Appendices
EVERDINGHE DEC 19th 1916	During the [crossed out] morning eleven 10 AM & 9.0 PM 9" 17" shells were fired into EVERDINGHE village.	
Dec 20th	During the afternoon the Bg air flew over hours of chayent on the enemy's trenches at the signal to the Infantry. At 1140 p.m. Gas S.O.S. Sgt Naston was received and the Bty + Battery fired 81 rounds of Shrapnel & H.E. rounds H.E. on S. of the front line trenches in the battery zone. Throughout the day the artillery was very active. Q the Bryan fired 110 rounds mostly in retaliation of enemy guns & trench mortars.	
Dec 21st	Misty day – bad light so that observation was impossible throughout the day. Enemy fired 40 rounds into Elverdinghe during the day.	

WAR DIARY
or
INTELLIGENCE SUMMARY

Army Form C. 2118

Place	Date	Hour	Summary of Events and Information	Remarks and references to Appendices
EVERDINGHE	22/12/15		Enemy fire was normal about 100 rounds being noted on the Regt Front. The Brigade did not fire all day.	
	23/12/15		Enemy active during the morning. 9th Battery destroyed a working party & established a c machine gun emplacement.	
	24/12/15		Enemy Artillery active during the morning 100 rounds being noted on the Bat Front. 8th Battery destroyed a party taking out their trenches & retaliated with 20 rounds for the shelling of EVERDINGHE by a high velocity gun. All was quiet during the evening.	
	25/12/15	6.0 pm	The Brigade took over the Front which had engaged since about noon. The previous day by the 9th Batty. Very in a working party at C.8.a.5.6. A working party at the Rway and on the ridge was also dispersed & numerous rounds fired at the enemy's parapet, about 50 rounds all told. The Enemy retaliated with 100 rounds at the 8th Battery position. B.5.c.10.4.	

Army Form C. 2118

Instructions regarding War Diaries and Intelligence Summaries are contained in F.S. Regs., Part II. and the Staff Manual respectively. Title Pages will be prepared in manuscript.

WAR DIARY
or
INTELLIGENCE SUMMARY
(Erase heading not required.)

Place	Date	Hour	Summary of Events and Information	Remarks and references to Appendices
ELVERDINGHE	26/12/15		The Enemy's Artillery was active during the day. The Bce. only fired on two points in the Enemy's line where movement was noticed. The fire was effective in each case.	
	27/12/15		Quiet day. A 5.9 Howitzer shell destroyed Ammunition Store at No 2 Gun Emplacement of the 6th Battery 13.15.C.10.H. and destroyed 20 rounds. Now 7 the Ammunition exploded.	
	28/12/15		Quiet day. We retaliated with 50 rounds H.E. for shelling of CHATEAU TROIS TOURS. 20 rounds of Shrapnel were fired on the enemies trenches with excellent effect in response to Infantry's call for retaliation. Officer Commanding Battery of 14th Division (A/46 & C/47 Battns.) took round our Captain Preparatory to taking them over from us.	
	29/12/15	6-24 P.M.	Came into S.O.S. E24 to E27. 110 rounds were fired in creating a barrage on the Centre Sector until fire lowered at 6-38 p.m.	
	30/12/15		ELVERDINGHE and vicinity was shelled intermittently throughout the day. About 200 rounds in all were fired exceeding 3-7". The weary Battery Commander of 14th Division arrived & verified our information during the afternoon. The section from our own battery	

1875 Wt. W593/826 1,000,000 4/15 J.B.C. & A. A.D.S.S./Forms/C. 2118.

Army Form C. 2118

WAR DIARY
or
INTELLIGENCE SUMMARY
(Erase heading not required.)

Instructions regarding War Diaries and Intelligence Summaries are contained in F.S. Regs., Part II. and the Staff Manual respectively. Title Pages will be prepared in manuscript.

Place	Date	Hour	Summary of Events and Information	Remarks and references to Appendices
	31/12/15		Were relieved by the 146th Divn. the guns being handed over to the relieving Sections in their emplacements, our position taken on the relieving Section Guns.	
	1/6		The remaining Section of each battery was withdrawn to the Wagon Lines taking on the relieving Section Guns, leaving them in the emplacements.	

John Taylor
Lieutenant Colonel V.D. R.F.A. (T.)
Commdg. 3rd. West Ridg. Bde. R.F.A. (T.)

247th (WR) Bde R.F.A
1/3rd West Riding Bde R.F.A.

War Diary ~ January 1916.
Dec 1 '16

Vol IX

+ Gn Lt L Duncan

WAR DIARY
or
INTELLIGENCE SUMMARY

Army Form C. 2118

Place	Date	Hour	Summary of Events and Information	Remarks and references to Appendices
OOSTHOEK.	1/6		The Brigade with Headquarters Coldry, Armour R28.b.2.9 at 6-30 a.m. started for the 8th 7th, & 9th Batteries, en route for the Rest Area. One NCO & two men were left in charge of each Battery Wagon Line near the expiration that the Brigade will return to this position after one month's rest. The route followed was Reninghe, Watou, Winnezeele, N of Hazebrouck N of Vieux-Cappel, Arneke, Rubrouck. The Brigade Column was left behind at its usual area at OOSTHOEK. The head of the Brigade reached the Tilin D'O 2 mile E of Rubrouck at 3-30 p.m. when it was met by the Battery Guides and the respective Battery Guards of Men were soon in their occupied lines dark.	
RUBROUCK	2/6		Very wet day.	
	3/6.		Dull day. C.R.A. 49th Division visited all the billets of the Brigade. Colonel P. Clynes V.D. left for 10 days leave in ENGLAND.	

Army Form C. 2118

WAR DIARY
or
INTELLIGENCE SUMMARY
(Erase heading not required.)

Place	Date	Hour	Summary of Events and Information	Remarks and references to Appendices
RUBROUCK	4/7/16		Fine day.	
	5/7/16		Wet day.	
	6/7/16		Wet day. Commence Battery Training. Team despatched by Brigade to escort Bryan Glemm and Sevenoak Ammunition Column (3rd Section) to Red Area.	
	7/7/16		Wet day. March into Red Area of Bryan & Sevenoak Ammunition Column postponed for one day.	
	8/7/16		Brigade Ammunition Column arrives at Viven D'a, 2 miles E.g. Rubrouck at 4-0 p.m. Where it was met by the Brigade Orderly Officer and conducted to its billets on the Westside of 2nd Lt F.G. Shattock Brucy Bryade R.F.G. on mile from the village	
	9/7/16		For day. Batteries attended 35th WFB3 England and respected to 7th Battery for service at RUBROUCK on Sutton	
	10/7/16		CHURCH first time out.	
	11/7/16		Fine day. Battery training	
	12/7/16		Fine day. Battery training	
	13/7/16		Wet day. Colonel C. Clifton returns from leave in ENGLAND	

WAR DIARY or INTELLIGENCE SUMMARY

Army Form C. 2118

Place	Date	Hour	Summary of Events and Information	Remarks and references to Appendices
ROUSBRUGGE	13/7/16		Fine day. Heavy Enemy shelling. Brigade Staff reconnoitred ground to N.N.E. of ESQUELBECQ and Brigade Position selected between ESQUELBECQ & WORMHOUT in connection with a scheme arranged by the Corps for the defence of 49th Division.	
	14/7/16		Fine day. Batteries found independently.	
	15/7/16		Dull Jersey day. Brigade is represented in Honours List by Major (Torpres) W. Mason, Capt. J. Cosgrove, Lieut. R.C. Bonn who have obtained the Military Cross. Col. Cooper and Bde Holland who have obtained the D.C.M. 2nd Lieuts J. Hepps, J. Armitage, and R.J. Carrll who are promoted to the rank of Lieut.	
	16/7/16		Fine day. Colonel inspected the Brigade Ammn.	
	17/7/16		Showery day. Brigade Staff & Battery Staffs were congratulated on their training.	
	18/7/16		Misty and dull necessitating the cancellation of the Brigade day which had been arranged.	
	19/7/16		Fine. Cold day. Batteries work independently.	

WAR DIARY
or
INTELLIGENCE SUMMARY

Army Form C. 2118

Place	Date	Hour	Summary of Events and Information	Remarks and references to Appendices
ROUBROUCK	20/7		Brigade route march, the head of column leaving THE VIOLIN D'OR at 9-30 A.M. Route due south to LEDERZEELE WAEMERS-CAPPEL road then west on BAVENBERG and turned North up the ROUBROUCK road.	
	21/7		Headquarters Staff & Battery Staffs go out in the morning in a scheme in nature of practice Inter-Communication. Two positions are taken up one behind the HOGEN HILL — HOFLAND and another behind the HERCKINGHEN - BOIZEELE road. The wired with wheel communication was established and was very satisfactory. Temp: Capt E.C. Clifford is promoted to be temporary Major & Lt Welby is promoted to be temporary Captain and transferred to 7th Battery.	
	22/7		Battery Staffs go out independently.	
	23/7		O.C. Brigade visits Head-Qrs of 17/78 A Battalion Reconnaissance Journal in the La BELLE VUE - WORMHOUT - ESQUELBECQ triangle to carried out by the Brigade	
	24/7			

WAR DIARY
or
INTELLIGENCE SUMMARY

Army Form C. 2118

(Erase heading not required.)

Place	Date	Hour	Summary of Events and Information	Remarks and references to Appendices
RUSROUCK	24/6		Battery Staffs to close O.P.s and fire positions in accordance with Bges. Scheme. In accordance with the scheme O.C. 3rd Bde. R.F.A.(?) was to move his Brigade to a position where FRENCH FYE 500 yards from the former Scene of the fight (r-1)-r and there at dawn await the army, find the ams had been ordered by an infantry V on F.O.O.s M.O. even in front of the 3rd Line...	
	25/6		Battery Staffs took arrangements In the L.S. Scheme to proceed to the 2nd Army Headquarters Signal Company and to struck picturing from 19th inst. Batteries took independently	
	26/6		Brigade and Battery Staffs have a communication scheme starting at Belenberg by S funnel and advance King's Redoubt on to Hospital ridge along the army line from 2nd Army Plumer, Commanding 2nd Army, General Caulfield, Artillery adviser.	
	27/6		Both General Percival Artillery adviser were with the Brigade during various scheme schemes	

WAR DIARY
or
INTELLIGENCE SUMMARY

Army Form C. 2118

Place	Date	Hour	Summary of Events and Information	Remarks and references to Appendices
ROBROUCK	28/6		Battery Parade. Brigade firing inspected by P.O.M. with view to extending the and gaining lessons of our hard war guns up to action at ELVERDINGHE. Officers, NCO's and men award decorations in recent offensives and presented with the decorations by General Plumer. Billeting Party leaves D.H.Q. G.O.D Brunston joined HQ. from 3/10 W.R. Bn R.A. Brigade prepare for its move. Nothing important.	
	29/6			
	30/6			
	31/6			

Jules St Pratt

Lieutenant Colonel V.D.R.F.A.(T)
Commdg. 3rd West Ridg. Bde. R.A.(T)

1/3rd West Riding Bde RFA

War Diary - February 1916.

Vol X

49th (W.R.) Division.

Vol 22

SECRET.

WAR DIARY.

OF

247th (wk) Brigade RFA

FOR

February 1917.

1916

Broken up

WAR DIARY
or
INTELLIGENCE SUMMARY

Army Form C. 2118

Place	Date	Hour	Summary of Events and Information	Remarks and references to Appendices
RUBROUCK	1/2/16		Nothing important	
	2/2/16		Nothing important	
	3/2/16		Brigade marches to BAVINCHOVE STATION to entrain for an unknown destination. Three train loads:—	
		9-31 A.M.	7th Battery and Section R. of the Ammunition Column	
		12-31 P.M.	8th Battery and Section of Headquarters & A.C.	
		3-31 P.M.	9th Battery and Section of Ammunition Column.	
			Detrainment of Brigade at LONGEAU at:—	
	4/2/16	9-31 P.M. – 12-31 A.M. – 3-30 A.M.	when it proceeds through AMIENS; AILLY-SUR-SOMME; PICQUIGNY; to HANGESTE-SUR-SOMME. Headquarters, 7th & 8th Batteries take up their billets in HANGESTE and Ammunition Column is put up fr the night; 9th Battery to accommodate for the by the 35th Brigade R.F.A. at BOURDON where their billets are arranged.	

WAR DIARY
or
INTELLIGENCE SUMMARY

Army Form C. 2118

Place	Date	Hour	Summary of Events and Information	Remarks and references to Appendices
HANGESTE SUR SOMME	5/2/16		9th Battery and Ammunition Column take up their billets at BOURDON. On the Guns evacuated by 33rd Brigade. C.O. visited billets. C.R.A. visited Brigade.	
	6/2/16		C.O. visited 9th Battery and Ammunition Column. C.O. went to a Conference at Divisional Head quarters in regard to a 4th Battery for Brigade and how it was to be raised and equipped.	
	7/2/16		Batteries at disposal of their O.C.'s	
	8/2/16		Batteries at disposal of their O.C.'s 2nd Lt J.G.J. Bord from Brigade from 3/1 D.A.C. and 2nd Lt R.J. Cahill transferred to Ammunition Column.	
	9/2/16		Batteries at disposal of their O.C.'s Church of England Service at 6.0 p.m. attended some 200 men this parade.	
	10/2/16		Bryden and Battery staff turn out on a Divisional Scheme the Various Guns employed in explaining the Scheme, & accompanying reports appendix for Batteries and Senior reports on to C.R.A.	

WAR DIARY
or
INTELLIGENCE SUMMARY

Army Form C. 2118

Place	Date	Hour	Summary of Events and Information	Remarks and references to Appendices
HARGESTE SUR SOMME	10/2/16		Afternoon was occupied in blowing up positions, laying out lines of fire etc. General Commander expressed his satisfaction at the way in which the scheme was carried out.	
	11/2/16		O.C. Brigade inspects horses of 7th Battery and attended a Conference of Brigade Commanders at C.R.A.'s office at HQ 901477	
	12/2/16		O.C. Brigade inspects 7th Battery Gun Park & stores. Gun Park 8th Battery & 9th Battery. 2 N.C.O.s are attached to the Brigade to instruct the Bde NCO's in the control of gun fire. 2nd Lieut. J. Jackson is posted to 8th Battery Lt. C. Warden " " 7th " Lt. G.J. Freeman " " 9th " 2nd Lt. G.J.J. Bond is attached to 8th Battery 2nd Lt. C.B. Bunton " " 9th Battery 2nd Lt. B.D. Parker is attached to 7th Battery for a fortnight. Course from 10 inst.	R.J.

WAR DIARY
or
INTELLIGENCE SUMMARY

Army Form C. 2118

Place	Date	Hour	Summary of Events and Information	Remarks and references to Appendices
HANGESTE	13/2/16	8.0 A.M.	Bryan's Bellotin Party moved up & mounted under Lt. J. Stiffs.	
		11-0 A.M.	Bryan Paraded for Gun Service.	
	14/2/16	5.30 A.M.	Bryan marches out of HANGESTE en route for VILLERS-BOCAGE via CROUY - AILLY-SAUVEUR - BERTANGLES. Head of Column reaches VILLERS-BOCAGE at 10-0 A.M. and Bryan billets there for night.	
	15/2/16	5.30 A.M.	Bryan marches out of HANGESTE arrives at HARPONVILLE via MOLLIENS-au-BOIS - BEAUCOURT - CONTAY. Head of Column reaches HARPONVILLE at 9-30 P.M. Artillery Hour. Bryan is billetted here in Divisional for an indefinite period. Lt. J. Stiffs is appointed Town Major of HARPONVILLE. Capt Saunders having departed on leave to ENGLAND Lt. J. Stiffs assumes the duties of acting Adjutant.	

Army Form C. 2118

WAR DIARY
or
INTELLIGENCE SUMMARY
(Erase heading not required.)

Place	Date	Hour	Summary of Events and Information	Remarks and references to Appendices
HARPON-VILLE	16/2/16		Units under their O.C.'s redres for a general clean up of billets, harness, Majority of men are put under shelter & the remainder on road mendings.	
	17/2/16		O.C. Bryan inspects 7th S, 8th & 9th Batteries.	
	18/2/16		Batteries go out to still run near the O.C.'s but return early on account of the heavy rain which continued throughout the day.	
	19/2/16		General clean up. Major Strom furis a lecture in the afternoon to all officers of the Brigade from notes which he had collected at the Senior Officers Course at BEAUVAL. Heavy firing was heard on our left at 6-0 p.m. for 3/4 hour.	
	20/2/16	10·30 AM	Lt-Col Crippi V.D. departs by motor car for a course at BEAUVAL. Senior Officers	
		1·0 PM	Church Parade at Protestant Church. HARPONVILLE.	

WAR DIARY
INTELLIGENCE SUMMARY

Army Form C. 2118

Place	Date	Hour	Summary of Events and Information	Remarks and references to Appendices
HARPONVILLE	21/2		Units at disposal of their O.C.s	
	22/2		Units at disposal of their O.C.s	
	23/2		Units at disposal of their O.C. Inoculation of men who have been over. Heavy snow storm.	
	24/2		60 men from Y.a Battery & 30 from 8a Battery go forward to Forfeau Sun Position for the Battery position. An stolen inspection near HAUTVILLET MARTINSART. They are provided with ants when they erect on the wind as there are no dug-outs or houses available.	
	25/2		Severe Blizzard prevents any work being done or sun position being constructed. Heavy snow which an endeavour is made to cover the sites by the emplacements and to smash the 8 men to work in daytime overseen by aeroplanes.	
	26/2		Colonel Clifford returns from BEAUVAL. Run Pool Bryan Taylor 18 4-hose teams to	

WAR DIARY
or
INTELLIGENCE SUMMARY

Army Form C. 2118

(*Erase heading not required.*)

Instructions regarding War Diaries and Intelligence Summaries are contained in F. S. Regs., Part II. and the Staff Manual respectively. Title Pages will be prepared in manuscript.

Place	Date	Hour	Summary of Events and Information	Remarks and references to Appendices
HARPONVILLE	26/16		Divisional Train to replace motor lorries. Rain falling the whole of notice. Cones ork man front or so received.	
	27/16		Church of England Service at Potatoes Church at HARPONVILLE. 18 4-inch Lams and 9 complements of 9 to 6pm Battery. Work done a complements of 9 to 6pm Battery. Eighteen 4-inch Lams again supplied to Divisional Train.	
	28/16		Work done a complements of 9 to 6pm Batteries. Eighteen 4-inch Lams are again supplied to Divisional Train.	
	29/16		Work done a complements of 9 YMP 6th Batteries and one of 8th Battery. Complements to forward Train etc-n.	

(signed) Gordon Thorpe
Lieutenant Colonel V.D. R.F.A.
Commdg. 3rd. West Ridg. Bde. R.F.A.

1/30 West Lancs Brig: R.F.A.

War Diary — March 1916.

Vol XI

49" (W.L.) Division

WAR DIARY
or
INTELLIGENCE SUMMARY
(Erase heading not required.)

Army Form C. 2118

Place	Date	Hour	Summary of Events and Information	Remarks and references to Appendices
HARPONVILLE	1/3/16		Battery parade in morning. Major General Percival CC Burem Inspected Brigade & afternoon & expressed his satisfaction of all he saw.	
	2/3/16	7.30pm	9th Battery relieves C.168 in action. Teams and Battery teams returns from Ammunition Column.	
	3/3/16		Turn out for Supply Column fatigues.	
	4/3/16		Staff N.H. men arrive for Bryan. Men for fatigues turn out again.	
	5/3/16		7th & 8th Batteries go into action, I am attached to the 48th Division Save Bizzard.	
	6/3/16		Notice of moving. Brigade Headquarters and Ammunition Column move into billets at MOLLIENS-AU-BOIS of which village Lt/Sgt Blake of Ammunition Column is appointed Town Major.	
MOLLIENS AU BOIS	7/3/16		Notice of intercut.	
	8/3/16		R.A. Band plays at MOLLIENS-AU-BOIS	
	9/3/16	2.30pm	Supply of 8 men arrive for Brigade	

1875 Wt. W593/825 1,000,000 4/15 J.B.C. & A. A.D.S.S./Form/C. 2118.

WAR DIARY or INTELLIGENCE SUMMARY

Army Form C. 2118

(Erase heading not required.)

Instructions regarding War Diaries and Intelligence Summaries are contained in F.S. Regs, Part II. and the Staff Manual respectively. Title Pages will be prepared in manuscript.

Place	Date	Hour	Summary of Events and Information	Remarks and references to Appendices
MOULIENS AU BOIS	10/3/16		Nothing of interest.	
	11/3/16		Nothing of interest.	
	12/3/16		Col Clifford assumes command of the Divisional Artillery on the departure of Brigadier General Caufield to England to take over Divisional area to held at Chateau of MOULIENS AU BOIS.	
	13/3/16	11.30 AM	Nothing of interest.	
	14/3/16		Nothing of interest.	
	15/3/16		Nothing of interest.	
	16/3/16		Orders from Division in all areas to be picketed in the open from this date.	
	17/3/16		Nothing of interest.	
	18/3/16		Reconnaissance of positions for Batteries in agenu of immediate exit in early retirement.	
	19/3/16	11.30 AM	Parade service at MOULIENS AU BOIS Chateau for Church of England. Reconnaissance of Battery positions in agenu of intermediate of Corps Line in case of a retirement. Also to the subsidiary Brigade in the scheme for the 32nd and 36th Divisions.	

Army Form C. 2118

WAR DIARY
or
INTELLIGENCE SUMMARY
(Erase heading not required.)

Instructions regarding War Diaries and Intelligence Summaries are contained in F. S. Regs., Part II and the Staff Manual respectively. Title Pages will be prepared in manuscript.

Place	Date	Hour	Summary of Events and Information	Remarks and references to Appendices
MOLLIENS AU BOIS.	20/3/16		Reconnaissance of battery positions for officers of Intendants & Cape Comn.	
	21/3/16		Leave recommenced for Time-expired men who have signed on for a further period of service. Reconnaissance of battery positions for officers of Intendants & Cape Comn.	
			Guns are issued to enable for Guns, Limbs, & Equipment for the 4th Battery who came for these from the Brigade. The Battery to Joins the Brigade as the A/y of 2nd RFA Brig. Rais. Battery.	
	22/3/16		All members of Brigade are directed by General Saghan Commander of Battery positions in defence of Interments & Cape Comn. D/S.J. Blake is temporarily transferred to 9th Battery pending return to England attached to temporary Commission Scheme.	
	23/3/16		Serving on actm in the early morning 9th Battery had 2 men killed & Lt Hayne & one man wounded.	
	24/3/16		Order for Major Jackson to proceed report to War Office in writing. 2nd Lieut Mygard to take over transferred to take Command of Brigade in the 2nd instance.	
	25/3/16		Nothing of interest.	
			Nothing of interest.	

Army Form C. 2118

WAR DIARY
or
INTELLIGENCE SUMMARY
(Erase heading not required.)

Instructions regarding War Diaries and Intelligence Summaries are contained in F.S. Regs., Part II. and the Staff Manual respectively. Title Pages will be prepared in manuscript.

Place	Date	Hour	Summary of Events and Information	Remarks and references to Appendices
MOLLIENS AU BOIS	26/6/3		Church Parade at 11.30 A.M. to Cancelled to account of a heavy first storm.	
	27/6/3		Lieut R.J. Cartt have been evacuated to ENGLAND to leave to the wharfs on 16th inst.	
	28/6/3		2nd Lt R. Reeves having joined the duty is posted to No. 1 Bryan. Ammunition Column with effect from 27th inst. Orders for movement of the Bryade, i.e. 1st, 8th, 9th & 49th Batteries to PERNOIS on 29th inst.	
	29/6/3		Bryade, i.e. 1st, 8th & 9th Batteries leave MOLLIENS-au-Bois at 11:30 A.M. and proceed to PERNOIS via VILLERS-BOCAGE, FLESELLES, HAVERNAS, HALLOY. Lt J. Staples behind with 1.M.C.O. & his men to clear up billets, and hand over to incoming units. Officers billets at PERNOIS all very good, mens' billets not so good, standings in known excellent. Every make of very early card tricks on the top of a farm slope.	
PERNOIS	30/6/3		Nothing to note. Sunny day	

1875 Wt. W593/826 1,000,000 4/15 J.B.C. & A. A.D.S.S./Forms/C. 2118.

WAR DIARY
or
INTELLIGENCE SUMMARY

(Erase heading not required.)

Army Form C. 2118

Instructions regarding War Diaries and Intelligence Summaries are contained in F. S. Regs., Part II. and the Staff Manual respectively. Title Pages will be prepared in manuscript.

Place	Date	Hour	Summary of Events and Information	Remarks and references to Appendices
PERNOIS	3/16/3		2nd Lt. O.R. Briggs having joined for duty is posted to the Brigade Ammunition Column. Hot, sunny day.	

Lieutenant Colonel V.D.R.F.A.
Commdg. 3rd West Ridg. Bdge. R.F.A.

To M.S. Bde A.B.A.

War Diary – April 1916

Vol XII

49th (W.R.) Division

X'n Corps

Place	Date	Hour	Summary of Events and Information	Remarks and references to Appendices
PERNOIS	1/4/16	4.30 pm	Right Section Ref 7th Battery under Lt Wardlow & 2nd Lt Shuttleworth left the Bivouac & is concentrated at BERTEAUCOURT.	
BERTEAU COURT.	2/4/16	9.30 AM 4.0 pm	Brigade Headquarters move into BERTEAUCOURT. 8th Battery, 9th Battery, remaining section of 7th Battery rejoin Brigade at BERTEAUCOURT. The horses of all these batteries had lost condition in considerably during their absence from the Brigade. Billets in BERTEAUCOURT and very good but there are no Forges here otherwise and the Ground is very soft. Majr G.H.W. Freebairn takes command Brigade, Lt Clifford still being acting CRA.	
	3/4/16		Nothing of interest.	
	4/4/16		Nothing of interest. Still unable to mount, in a the horses of for other and men at Headquarters & B.a.C. 26 per battery. A course of Sun Drill to commenced for instruction of the many Battery Joined Officers of the Bde. 2nd Lt Shuttleworth, 2 Lt Wilmers; 6.9. F. Reid; C.D. Bruton; N.C. Jato; R. Burrows; 8	
	5/4/16			
	6/4/16			

Army Form C. 2118

WAR DIARY
or
INTELLIGENCE SUMMARY
(Erase heading not required.)

Instructions regarding War Diaries and Intelligence Summaries are contained in F.S. Regs., Part II. and the Staff Manual respectively. Title Pages will be prepared in manuscript.

Place	Date	Hour	Summary of Events and Information	Remarks and references to Appendices
BERTEAU-COURT	7/4/16	2-30 pm	Enumeration of Establishments. Brigade Orders dated L.G. operation Order. Reduction of rising two [?] Ammunition Column who are now Corps Major &c. to the New Army Establishment.	
	8/4/16			
	9/4/16	9-30 pm	Left N. Gardens departs to England to report to War Office on Ammunition with Major to 2nd Line. Signal Service.	
	10/4/16		L/Cpl O. Potts attached to 8th Battery. L/Cpl J. Shuttleworth to take over the duties of Mr. Major Graf of animated animals arrives. All [Squadrons] or B.W.'s Hqs Commencement of Special training to enter communication centres.	
	11/4/16		As to divert six tons per day to [Squadron] Hqs work with Battery and B.m. Staffs ext. afternoon. First day for return to Ordnance of all worn Clothing.	
	12/4/16		Scale of Stud limits increased to 26 per Battery	
	13/4/16		22 L.D. & J. News arrive for the Brigade.	
	14/4/16		Nothing of interest.	
			Confirmation Service at Naours.	
	15/4/16		Nothing of interest	

G.H.

WAR DIARY
or
INTELLIGENCE SUMMARY
(Erase heading not required.)

Army Form C. 2118

Place	Date	Hour	Summary of Events and Information	Remarks and references to Appendices
BERTEAU-COURT	16/4	9:30 AM	Church Service at Hoogersten. Remount of 14th M.P. Battery arriving & 2nd/Reserve	
	17/4		Batteries at disposal of O.C. in moving to Hawerincy & Busny Stall. Issues of Battery stops in afternoon prepared by Battery Commanders. 25 N.C.O.s & men of new battery in attached to each of 7th & 14th M.P. Bdes. for Gunnery Purposes. Officer Infantry Correspondence with Staynor [?] inclosing adverbisements [?] "Staynor". Bior awer [?] for all units to moving. Battery staff in reserve prepared by Battery Commanders. Ran on Question & Solution. Exercise round WARGAMES — CRA treated Bde & Ghost Forces known "ARMY". The C's instruction of 7th 8th & 9th Batteries have been referred to the 14th M.P. Battery. These would each consist of 3 Subs. 1 Capt, 2 Subs, 1 a/B., 1 B., 1 S/Mjr., 9 Gunners (Gun teams, Gun Battery), 9	
	18/4			
	19/4		1st Line Major) "Capt G.N. Fenton will take over command of the 1st M.P. Battery with effect from to-day."	

WAR DIARY or INTELLIGENCE SUMMARY

Army Form C. 2118

Place	Date	Hour	Summary of Events and Information	Remarks and references to Appendices
BERTEAU COURT	20/4/16	2.0 p.m.	Bde Exercise in afternoon — ready trans Sgt J.B. to BERTEAUCOURT. All officers including 14th NM Battery Officers told attend. O.C. & Sgt. 6 in & J to place who knew few Battery at disposal. & O.C. 14th NM Battery.	
	21/4/16		2 Sgt Barnes 9 Lance NCOs & men are attached to 146th NM Battery. The new Battery will in future be known as D.3. WM Battery Organised. Tactical Exercise at WARGNIES with 148th Inf. Bn on ground marked out to represent trenches. Capt G N Fortin and take over Command of D.3 Battery with effect from 18th instant.	
	22/4/16		All Batteries the Brigade held in morning. Comm: Col Jes Jen Route March. Bgde & Battery Staff Carryout exercise in Mounted Return.	
VIGNACOURT & BERTEAUCOURT	23/4/16		EASTER SUNDAY. Communion celebrated in 5th Battery billet at 9 a.m.	
	24/4/16		Sgt G Helps resumes his duties as Orderly Officer at 10 a.m. Sgt.	

WAR DIARY
or
INTELLIGENCE SUMMARY
(Erase heading not required.)

Army Form C. 2118

Place	Date	Hour	Summary of Events and Information	Remarks and references to Appendices
BERTEAU COURT	25/4	8.15am	Brigade & Battery Staffs ready — ordered to take post in a tactical exercise with 148th Bty. 15a.c. MARGNIES. Our personnel marched out as tactical officers of D.3. and attached to 7th, 8th and 9th Batteries for this purpose. 2/Lt. Blake to posted to 9th Battery. 2/Lt. Ramsay to posted to D.3 Battery. Smith, Shelton & Stainey Arrive and posted to the 9th and 8th Batteries respectively. Manœuvring and Gun Drill for all batteries in morning. Bde & Battery staffs exercised in inter-communication in fernoon in vicinity of ST LEGER & DOMART.	
	26/4		2nd pt Gun Drill. Pm horses from D.3 Battery for Art-Aarey.	
	27/4		Guns still in Armoury. D.3 in rear and Gun Drill. 21 horses and 9 mules arrive in evening. Made many of light duty at unload afternoon. Other horses need rest all unfit.	

Army Form C. 2118

WAR DIARY
or
INTELLIGENCE SUMMARY
(Erase heading not required.)

Instructions regarding War Diaries and Intelligence Summaries are contained in F. S. Regs., Part II. and the Staff Manual respectively. Title Pages will be prepared in manuscript.

Place	Date	Hour	Summary of Events and Information	Remarks and references to Appendices
BERTEAU COURT	28/4/16		Brigade Cmdt. Majors Bryan & R.H. Trippett Adjts. and 2 Company Officers attached to Am. Cl. on duty.	
	29/4/16		Recog-mce of Bryan and Battery staffs at Pozieres when necessary communications carried on until 10 p.m.	
	30/4/16		Pozieres Service for all units at Bar HQ 9.15 a.m. 9-30 a.m. at Bar HQ Headquarters.	

J. Harris (?)
Lieutenant Colonel R.D.R.F.A.
Commdg. 3rd West Ridg. Bdge. R.F.A.

1875 Wt. W593/826 1,000,000 4/15 J.B.C. & A. A.D.S.S./Forms/C. 2118.

MAY/JUNE MISSING

✓ WHEN MARKING UP DOCUMENTS FOR COPYING PLEASE TICK THE APPROPRIATE BOX ON THE OPPOSITE SIDE OF THIS MARKER. THIS INFORMATION IS ESSENTIAL TO ALLOW US TO PROVIDE YOU WITH THE COPIES YOU REQUIRE INFORMATION SHEETS ARE AVAILABLE FROM THE RECORD COPYING COUNTER SHOULD YOU NEED FURTHER ASSISTANCE. ************************************

49th. DIVISIONAL ARTILLERY

247th. BRIGADE R. F. A.

SEPTEMBER 1916.

49

R 17

34th (M.D) Bn Aza

War Diary — Sept 1916

Army Form C. 2118

WAR DIARY
or
INTELLIGENCE SUMMARY
(Erase heading not required.)

Instructions regarding War Diaries and Intelligence Summaries are contained in F.S. Regs., Part II. and the Staff Manual respectively. Title Pages will be prepared in manuscript.

Place	Date	Hour	Summary of Events and Information	Remarks and references to Appendices
Q22c120 (FRANCE) 57°SE 1/25000	1/9/16.		Assault again postponed for 24 hours. Bethune. Continue to keep Enemy wire open. Weather still very bad.	
	2/9/16.		Assault again postponed for 24 hours. Bethune. Continue to keep wire to an Law open.	
	3/9/16.	5-10 am	Intense Bombardment (20 per attached programme of operations) commences	
		5-13 am	Assault takes place.	
		11-0 am	Enemy aeroplanes flying over. Artillery Activity.	
		11-30 am	Shelling by Artillery commences and the following casualties occur:— 6/243 1 killed 4/248 1 wounded 1 wounded	

WAR DIARY or INTELLIGENCE SUMMARY

Army Form C. 2118

Place	Date	Hour	Summary of Events and Information	Remarks and references to Appendices
Q22.c.10.20. (FRANCE) (57D S.E.) (1/20,000)	3/9.		Events during Operations	
		8.29 am	Enemy reported retiring at R19.d.28. A/246 fire then 3 rounds Gun fire followed by Battery fire 6" fire 5 minutes and then 10 minutes at Rate Gun minute	
		8.33 am	C/243 also ordered to quicken rate of fire to 1 round per gun per minute	
		8.38 am	(Ratio increased all round on battery zones in phase 3 fire orders attached) by order of CRA.	
		8.46 am	A/246 reduced to slower rate of fire to 1 round-gun-minute	
		8.54 am	Bryan Major reports Counter attack developing from SCAMPSON REDOUBT. Ratio of fire on zones increased to 2 round gun-minute	
		8.55 am	A/246 ordered to return The "target" in phase 3 (Operation Order)	
		9.0 am	C/243 reports hostile plane fire then previous without hindrance	
		9.25 am	A/246 reports about 20 men identity unknown at R19.c.13.20.	
		9.35 am	Fire reduced to one round-gun- 2 minutes by order of CRA	

WAR DIARY or INTELLIGENCE SUMMARY

Army Form C. 2118

Place	Date	Hour	Summary of Events and Information	Remarks and references to Appendices
O.22.c.10.20. (FRANCE 57D SE)	3/9/16	9.35 am	We report that we are getting short of Ammunition.	
		9.40 am	A/242 reports 1 gun out of action and all Saddles Strain of Sustained heavy firing.	
		10-7 am	A/242 an reserved to Cease firing owing to shortage of Ammunition. They only had 250 rounds left and it was thought advisable to save this for emergencies.	
		10-8 am	Our Infantry reported falling back to our line and on their way to barrage the front from Faveulls	
		10-17 am	E.R.A. Gregario A/248 to fire on Track R19a04-R19a30 at 2 rounds per gun per minute for 5 minutes.	
		10-20 am	Capt Taylor reports Boche leaving Stanfohr Lynis w/ R14a66.	
		10-23 am	A/248 ordered to Cease firing & to be ready for any thing	
		10-47 am	A/248 reports men coming down communication trench to R19c25.	

WAR DIARY
or
INTELLIGENCE SUMMARY
(Erase heading not required.)

Army Form C. 2118

Place	Date	Hour	Summary of Events and Information	Remarks and references to Appendices
B22c0120 (FRANCE) 57 SE 1/20000	3/16	10.51 am	Ask B11RA for supervision from troops.	
		10.53 am	A7&6 returned to fire on enemy coming into R19c28. At 5 rounds per gun-minute until exhausted and afterwards at slow rate on own section of support line.	
		10.55 am	Ordered all batteries to turn on to phase 2	
		10.56 am	O.P.A. informs us bursts of fire on front & support lines.	
		10.58 am	Reported to O.R.A. Ammunition on hand at 10.30 am & it was of phase. Sun 17 H Guns D H 175 abo per each " 17 H " BA 79 " 4 " PE 265 " 6 " PG 150 " 6 "	
		11.13 am	Reduced rate of fire to 1/4 rd per gun per minute owing to shortage of ammunition. Apx 6 report that D.A.C. has run out.	

Army Form C. 2118

WAR DIARY
or
INTELLIGENCE SUMMARY
(Erase heading not required.)

Place	Date	Hour	Summary of Events and Information	Remarks and references to Appendices
Q22C1020 FRANCE 57 B.E. (1/20000)	3/6/17	11-15 am	O.P.A. Observer Southern to Sprinkle Wounds about i.e. from both 1 to 2 to 3 to 1 to 2 etc.	
		11-18 am	Capt Septon reports party of men going from R19a 45 53 to 6030 and hith up trench	
		11-45 am	Small parties of enemy walking down trench R19a 35 and R19c 36 and appear to be making for R19a 00.	
		11-45 am	A/246 reports 50 men entered enemy front line " "	
		4-20 pm	A/246 reports further 40 men " " "	
		4-22 pm	O.C. C/243 reports numbers of men seen along C.T.s from R19a 6025 to R19c 38 support trench.	
		7-30 pm	Rounds from each gun of all batteries on or near gun to enemy front line also neared on target of report from A/246 that real numbers of enemy can be seen in his front line.	

WAR DIARY or INTELLIGENCE SUMMARY

Army Form C. 2118

Place	Date	Hour	Summary of Events and Information	Remarks and references to Appendices
Q.22 c10 20. (FRANCE 57D SE) (1:20000)	3/9/16	10-0 pm	Enemy commenced to shell Q.16 & vicinity with Lachrymatory shells. Appears that Bn occupying keyless open was in the trench support trenches of Enemy commenced to shell area from AUCHONVILLERS to MESNIL with gas shells, many concentrating on the flanks of RASTOFF with gas shells.	
	4/9/16	12-15 am	On East, Stein Redoubt just short of dug out and extra Orderly Officers Dug out but beyond trenches down to work nothing to the Bay of damage is done. A/242 B/243 } gas fired Bn. stand to Repairing open wire in the enemy Leipzig Area } from trench on THIEPVAL - LEIPZIG SALIENT. A/242 Shells area Q.22 and Q.26. A/243 } Been employing as putty well as they can all day. Enemy Artillery very active 8 gunch 8 inch & 10 inch A/245 fired onto LEIPZIG & THIEPVAL storage A/242, A/245 C/243 3	
	5/9/16		Wet weather. Returned 4 all night patrol	

WAR DIARY
or
INTELLIGENCE SUMMARY
(Erase heading not required.)

Army Form C. 2118

Instructions regarding War Diaries and Intelligence Summaries are contained in F.S. Regs., Part II. and the Staff Manual respectively. Title Pages will be prepared in manuscript.

Place	Date	Hour	Summary of Events and Information	Remarks and references to Appendices
Q22 e1020 (FRANCE 57DSE 1/20000)	6/9/16	2.0 pm	Enemy shells nearly bombarded of CHARLES AVENUE vigorously. Orders are received for Battery J Enfield Rings to leave their positions in action under a Guard and to concentrate the Platoons at the Chateau down for a few days. Batter for the Group H.Q. to Return to VARENNES.	
		5.30pm	Group H.Q. moves to VARENNES.	
VARENNES	7/9/16	4.00am	Enemy shells VARENNES - no damage done to us. Heavy Artillery bombardment pitches all day. The battle Intensive bombardment still intend.	
	8/9/16		Many Enemy Balloons with Automatic Samples destruction fuses are seen. Meta Corp ordered for Group J Battery Hqrs run into AMIENS for a day off. Returning to VARENNES at 7-0pm.	
	9/9/16 10-0 am		day off. Anthony J Dubuit.	[signature]
	10/9/16	"	Commence Signalling - visual - for the next day	
	11/9/16	"	" Visual	
	12/9/16	"	" Visual	
	13/9/16	"	" Visual	
	14/9/16	"	" Visual	

Army Form C. 2118

WAR DIARY
or
INTELLIGENCE SUMMARY
(Erase heading not required.)

Instructions regarding War Diaries and Intelligence Summaries are contained in F. S. Regs., Part II and the Staff Manual respectively. Title Pages will be prepared in manuscript.

Place	Date	Hour	Summary of Events and Information	Remarks and references to Appendices
VARENNES	15/9/16		Commenced work on horse standings — Natural albout soil Chalk and rough timber.	
			Received news of the fall of COURCELETTE — FLERS — MARTIN PUICH HIGH WOOD — BOULEAUX WOOD. Also rumoured that LES BOEUFS and in our hands and that we are advancing on to GUEUDECOURT.	
			ACHEUX dump shelled.	
	16/9/16		Seven September day — bright sun with a cool breeze. Quite a quiet day.	
			Two of our German aeroplanes ten minutes one after the innernings and one fired at by Anti-aircraft gun but no attention by our machines.	S.A.
	17/9/16		Another quiet day. One solitary German aeroplane came over at a high altitude about 5000 feet and is shelled by Anti-aircraft in of our machines rose to give battle but carry to the Superior height he found rapidly on him.	
	18/9/16		Fearful day — Pours with rain.	

Army Form C. 2118

WAR DIARY
or
INTELLIGENCE SUMMARY
(Erase heading not required.)

Instructions regarding War Diaries and Intelligence Summaries are contained in F.S. Regs., Part II. and the Staff Manual respectively. Title Pages will be prepared in manuscript.

Place	Date	Hour	Summary of Events and Information	Remarks and references to Appendices
VARENNES.	18/9/16		Weather breaks and we have an appalling day.	
	19/9/16		Another wet day. Note above on horse shooting's between the shower.	
	20/9/16		Wet day again.	
	21/9/16		Prior again. Received oars to relieve Col. White 2/6th Bn H.D. at midday on 22 st and take command of his Regt Group.	
MESNIL.	22/9/16		Take over Left Group from Colonel White consisting of the following Batteries.	
			A/248 Commanded by Capt Tyler.	
			B/248 " " Major Bullock D.S.O. T.D.	
			C/241 " " Major Thompson.	
			A/246 " " Major Ashton.	
			B/246 " " Major Pearing.	
			D/248. " " Major Duncan D.S.O.	
			Sons and all Standards Officers who were left on under Colonel White.	

WAR DIARY
or
INTELLIGENCE SUMMARY
(Erase heading not required.)

Army Form C. 2118

Instructions regarding War Diaries and Intelligence Summaries are contained in F. S. Regs., Part II. and the Staff Manual respectively. Title Pages will be prepared in manuscript.

Place	Date	Hour	Summary of Events and Information	Remarks and references to Appendices
Q.28a.9.3.	23/6 9/9		Comparatively clear day.	
57DSE 1/20000	24/6 9/9		G.O.C. Division General Pereira called round to the O.C and visits all batteries.	
	25/6 9/9		Registration finished. South of THIEPVAL from the LEIPZIG SALIENT. Thient to flank covis firing up the LEFT & CENTRE GROUPS. and CENTRE and RIGHT GROUPS. Very unsatisfactory as own are not at all good told to manage somehow. Further registration and a twenty shar day for it.	
	26/6 9/9	12.35 pm	The bombardment commenced according to attached copy of news. The barrage commenced as from 1.5am and worked on tentatively on clear & held against G.f.b. All our information was received from the O.P.s and we were continuously keeping in. col Whitby, Liaison Officer with Infantry with information for as usual to A.P's Att Pts Bde Bde Battle HQrs knew his stuff.	S

1875 Wt. W 593/826 1,000,000 4/15 J.B.C. & A. A.D.S.S./Forms/C.2118.

WAR DIARY
or
INTELLIGENCE SUMMARY
(Erase heading not required.)

Army Form C. 2118

Instructions regarding War Diaries and Intelligence Summaries are contained in F.S. Regs., Part II. and the Staff Manual respectively. Title Pages will be prepared in manuscript.

Place	Date	Hour	Summary of Events and Information	Remarks and references to Appendices
Q28a93 5ᴅSE. 1/20000	26/9/16		The enemy barrage was feeble and created without any harassment. By nightfall we knew how our left flank was situated but had no idea what had happened E of R26a 2.3 and indeed never did find out.	
	27/9/16		Our line was advanced to R25.t 34, to R25.t.88 before nightfall but as we found on that the infantry were very thin on the ground except at points, an attempt was made to fill the gaps. Patrols were sent out for reconnaissance.	
		4pm	Orders recd for bombardment & a further attempt on the SCHWABEN REDOUBT but this was postponed until 28th.	
	28/9/16		Assault of SCHWABEN at 1.0 P.M. Barrage was good but information failed on OP's. Could not see more than the nearest edge and so really never knew how the Western Enemy Communication Trench Valley at 10-50pm with KASTOFF and LACHRYMATORS accompanied by G.T.9" H.E.	JR

WAR DIARY
or
INTELLIGENCE SUMMARY
(Erase heading not required.)

Army Form C. 2118

Place	Date	Hour	Summary of Events and Information	Remarks and references to Appendices
Q26093 57D3E 1/20000	29/9/16	2-15 am	Enemy Feuev fire on the trolley. Fire too certain. Posted guns efficient so that it was not necessary to fire as it was S'nothe blunts. Any one it were S'nothe blunts.	
	30/9/16	6-30 am	Counter attack on the SCHWABEN REDOUBT. Absolutely no information. So not for fluctuate between S.O.S. and normal until 7-25am when an S.O.S settled down to S.O.S. but have to carry on at reduced rates of fire owing to shortage of ammunition. Remainder of Ag'v'o Compensatory Gun. C/241 v0 relieved by B/85- and B/246 relieved by battery of 51st Division. A/246, B/246, A/246 and D/246 left Jury have on section relieved	

[signature]

2/1 (M.D) Bde A.A. (49 Div)

Vol 18

War Diary - October 1916

49th Div

C.E.F.

Army Form C. 2118

WAR DIARY
or
INTELLIGENCE SUMMARY
(Erase heading not required.)

Instructions regarding War Diaries and Intelligence Summaries are contained in F.S. Regs., Part II. and the Staff Manual respectively. Title Pages will be prepared in manuscript.

Place	Date	Hour	Summary of Events and Information	Remarks and references to Appendices
Q28 c93. 57D SE 1/20000.	1/10/16	5-50 am	S.O.S. SCHWABEN REDOUBT. Bottom very low with ammunition so that for hour & fire at normal rate. However it turns out to be a false alarm and was probably due to a sentry fight in the N.W. face of the redoubt. Company day. Battery ships are employed with 51st Div. S.O.S. again but no one knows where & why and the soon over.	
	2/10/16	6-1 am		
		12-0 midday	Wear relieved at midday by Genl. Staton Commanding 260th Bde 51st Div. and we proceed to VARENNES. At midnight we move rations to move to GROUCHES via ACHEUX - LEALVILLERS - LOUVENCOURT - MARIEUX - ORVILLE at 5-30 am. on 3/10/16. Passing near Marieul at 6-30 am. but are delayed just outside VARENNES	
VARENNES LENS 1/10000 Sheet 11	3/10/16		by numerous "tanks" which are being unloaded from the train and have managed to get stuck in the middle of the road.	

1875 Wt. W593/826 1,000,000 4/15 J.B.C. & A. A.D.S.S./Forms/C. 2118.

Army Form C. 2118

WAR DIARY
or
INTELLIGENCE SUMMARY
(Erase heading not required.)

Instructions regarding War Diaries and Intelligence Summaries are contained in F.S. Regs., Part II. and the Staff Manual respectively. Title Pages will be prepared in manuscript.

Place	Date	Hour	Summary of Events and Information	Remarks and references to Appendices
GROUCHES LENS 1/10000 Sheet 11	3/10/16	11.0 am	Arrive GROUCHES and manage fairly for accomodation. Shelters are to own of men and horses for officers are very muddy.	
	4/10/16	9.0 am	Leave near 8th road at 9.0 am to LAHERLIERE via LUCHEUX, SAULTY. Billeting party in arrived find that accommodation for an mess and that there is very accommodation for an party of Brigade which is being billeted in LAHERET. After conversation time with secretaire of DRBMG of 16th Divison we felt forced up at 2.30pm with another first visited GOUY-en-PRETOIS and later Lo tints for the divisions officers and remainder of men are accomodated 2 miles away in Southern edge of BAVINCOURT in huts/tents.	

1875 W. W593/826 1,000,000 4/15 J.B.C. & A. A.D.S.S./Forms/C. 2118.

Army Form C. 2118

WAR DIARY
or
INTELLIGENCE SUMMARY
(Erase heading not required.)

Instructions regarding War Diaries and Intelligence Summaries are contained in F. S. Regs., Part II. and the Staff Manual respectively. Title Pages will be prepared in manuscript.

Place	Date	Hour	Summary of Events and Information	Remarks and references to Appendices
BAVINCOURT	5/10/16	9-20 am	Recc'd order fr. O.C. Bde. with Lt. Adjutant & and O.R.A. at Church at SOUASTRE at 11-0 am fr. purpose of making a reconnaissance. Lt. Colonel Charles Appia, O.C. Bde., on being given command 180th Infantry Bde. attached to Defence Troops ordered B company to man gallery at E26 a 50 40, by O.C. 2/4th St Bde. and on section B/248 situated at E8 b 60 20, and on section B/D247 at E8 a 20 20 and to report with fr. defence g D/247 at E11c91 to K3a16 from 10am on morning of 9/10/16.	
FRANCE 57DNE 1/20,000	6/10		Proceed to BIENVILLERS & occupy our Headquarters at E8 a 20 20. One section of D/247 under Command of Lt. BLOEM forward Cotton at E8a 1020	S.H.

WAR DIARY or INTELLIGENCE SUMMARY

Army Form C. 2118

Place	Date	Hour	Summary of Events and Information	Remarks and references to Appendices
BIENVILLERS (FRANCE 57D NE.) (1/20000)	6/10/16		One Section of B/245 under Major Bullock came into action at E8c6010	
	7/10/16		One Section of B/245 under Major Lucy came into action at E26a4060. Nothing of interest.	
	8/10/16		Nothing of interest.	
	9/10/16	10.00am	Remaining Section of B/246 & B/245 came into action. Taken over defence of line from E11c91 to E28c21 = supporting 141st Infantry Brigade which relieved 148th during the day. Recce news to return to Major Lucy after landing over D/247 and B/246 to O.C. 246th 13dv. Over 13/245 to O.C. 245-13dv.	
	10/10/16	4-3.30pm	Stand over and return to Major Lucy.	
		5-0pm	On late Headquarters at BIENVILLERS partially strongly for further.	
GOUY-en-ARTOIS (LENS Sheet 11) (1/10000)	11/10/16		And 2 men of D/247 and 1 sent from it wounded by shell fire and Sgt D. Wight slightly but on duty. Officer called out food – but nothing to report about in accommodation & Am. Water supply, no trouble in this Billety. Staff Sgt Fitter M'Nutt Signaller J.J. and 6 men are employed for	

1375 W.W.593/826 4,000,000 7/4/15 J.B.C. & A. A.D.S.S./Forms/C.2118/5.

WAR DIARY
or
INTELLIGENCE SUMMARY

(Erase heading not required.)

Army Form C. 2118

Place	Date	Hour	Summary of Events and Information	Remarks and references to Appendices
GOUY-EN-ARTOIS	11/10/16		12 hours out of the 24 Journeying in reliefs. Shelters are very muddy. Staff Sergt Tutin MITCHELL and G. wounded.	
(LENS Sheet 11 1/100000)	12/10/16		Nothing of note. Weather still bad.	
	13/10/16		Again nothing of note — Weather remains uncertain.	
	14/10/16		Snowing by this day. General KAY D.S.O. (CRA) call round during morning to see Batting lines, and to tell us that he an about to move into 2. 6pm 15pm Batteries and 1 4.5 Howzr on Batting position and 1 Conference at CRA's Offs with reference to reorganisation of Divisional Artillery.	
	15/10/16		Major Mc-Garneston of B.M. was sent out after a conference of Colonel with 18 Pdr Batting Commanders when it is decided to form up B/247 (late 8th (HR) Battery) Commanded by Capt Trent, Temporary Capt, F.W. Gent handing over section to rest of A/C.	[signature]

WAR DIARY
or
INTELLIGENCE SUMMARY

(Erase heading not required.)

Army Form C. 2118

Instructions regarding War Diaries and Intelligence Summaries are contained in F.S. Regs., Part II. and the Staff Manual respectively. Title Pages will be prepared in manuscript.

Place	Date	Hour	Summary of Events and Information	Remarks and references to Appendices
Bouv-en-Artois (Lens Sht 11 1/100000)	16/10/16	2-3.30pm	Orders received for entrainment of 1st section of A, B, C, & D Batteries to-night, the remaining Section to entrain on night of 17th-18th. All ammunition to begin train to be taken by D.A.C. and begun of entire to rept at Jun dumps. D.A.C. removing remainder of dumps.	
	17/10/16		Orders received to trek to Bus-en-Artois at 9-0 am on morning 18th via Bainecourt – Lahrbret – La Bezeque – Fne – St Amand – Souastre – Couin. Colonel goes with C.R.A. to reconnoitre positions. 2nd Section of Batteries gone out of action. Wet day as usual when we march.	
	18/10/16	8-15 am 9-0 am	Brigade marches under command of Capt P.M. Stout for Bus OP Bde with OC Batteries, Adjutant, & Orderly Officer go forward in motor lorry to reconnoitre battery positions. It is found that many of dug-outs need to extend as 17 tons	S.H.

1375 Wt. W.593/825 1,000,000 4/15 J.B.C. & A. A.D.S.S./Forms/C.2118.

WAR DIARY
or
INTELLIGENCE SUMMARY

Army Form C. 2118

Place	Date	Hour	Summary of Events and Information	Remarks and references to Appendices
Bus-en-ARTOIS (LENS Sheet 11) (1/10000)	18/1/16		Have been occupied by somone the during my tb. There are not any positions prepared and accomodation for personnel is practically nil.	
		6.0pm	Watch on So on to Bus-en-ARTOIS when we are to have our wagon lines. Roads are fearfully congested with Caterpillars during by knoxgens. Ammunition lorries, 9 horse transport so that it takes us over an hr to go from MAILLY-MAILLET to BUS-en-ARTOIS. Billets for men are not too bad, billets for officers are in a very ricketty hut with round from and no doors.	
		6.50pm	O.P.A. arrives and informs us that day's work is a wash-out and we are to be rundered over to 3rd Division. So we make an appointment for the morn.	[signature]

WAR DIARY
INTELLIGENCE SUMMARY
(Erase heading not required.)

Army Form C. 2118

Place	Date	Hour	Summary of Events and Information	Remarks and references to Appendices
BUS-on-ARTOIS (Lens Sheet II 1/100000)	19/10/16		Met C.R.A. 7th Bde. A.V.th Bde. Headquarters COURCELLES to new position and upon J. Partially prepared C-gun 18 pdr position and 1.4.5 How position. B.C.'s & turned to reconnoitre new position and Colonel and C.R.A. So on the Battery position and Brigade H.Q. Dug into an almost nightjar except for 'C' Battery close accommodation is in BASIN WOOD. Battery position & H.Q. as so under. 247th Brigade H.Q. — Lt Colonel Clifford V.D. — K.26.f.6.3. A/247th Battery — Lt (temporary Major) J.C. Clifford — K.27.f.50.70. B/247th Battery — Lt ( ) W. Amison MC. K.28.c.50.30. D/247th Battery — Capt Tennison RA. K.27.f.9.5. Battery start work on the Gun-position with a Part.—harness On 3rd Division RE. Dump at COURCELLES.	
	20/10/16		Keen frost in morning	J.H.

WAR DIARY
or
INTELLIGENCE SUMMARY

(Erase heading not required.)

Army Form C. 2118

Instructions regarding War Diaries and Intelligence Summaries are contained in F. S. Regs., Part II. and the Staff Manual respectively. Title Pages will be prepared in manuscript.

Place	Date	Hour	Summary of Events and Information	Remarks and references to Appendices
COURCELLES	20/10 to 21/10		E Bar A.B. Bryan. Move into billets in COURCELLES. Rain fired in early morning. Battery took to Farm Lycation. A. HELPS slightly burned by premature? 9 ————— Moments at duty. All officers and men are accomodated in shelter tents. Made room for Infantry, and as a result of this billets in Bus to	
LENS Sheet 11 1/10000	22/10		Beginning problem. Yours - truly. Opened X day	
	23/10		Ran first to ranging. Batter postponed. QH has Operation Order. Recur Ammunition to into action. Battery Neighs Gnr J Duncan E' battery killed by a Shell and No 1005 Gnr A Smith Was slightly wounded. This Incident occurred in Basin Wood.	
	24/10	8-10 pm	Thiepval. Lt Armitage awarded Military Cross for Good work at Thiepval. Vuy 1st May I Any postponed until 28th inst.	

WAR DIARY or INTELLIGENCE SUMMARY

Army Form C. 2118

Place	Date	Hour	Summary of Events and Information	Remarks and references to Appendices
COURCELLES (LENS) Sheet 11 (1/100000)	25/10/16		'C' Battery expels northern edge of PENDANT COPSE with 7 rounds. Battery Commanders return to wagon lines in evening. Wear reported that 576th H.S. Howitzer Battery is posted to us and has arrived at HAVRE. This Battery has orders to join D.A.C. until further known. Operation is Orr. No. 906. Lt. F. Shearman, 'A' Battery, wounded in back by a machine gun bullet and subsequently died. Very wet day.	
	26/10/16	12.30pm	1 day postponed until 30th. General Kay D.S.O. visit all batteries positions. Enemy airplanes very active all day. And his guns play on our front system all afternoon. It seems that he has, J.D. brought up many more guns — at anyrate he volume of fire has increased immensely.	

WAR DIARY
or
INTELLIGENCE SUMMARY
(Erase heading not required.)

Army Form C. 2118

Place	Date	Hour	Summary of Events and Information	Remarks and references to Appendices
COURCELLES (LENS Sheet 11 1/40000)	27/16 /10		Continuous rain. Nothing of interest.	
	28/16 /10		1- day preferred to 30th inst.	
	29/16 /10		518th battery, commanded by Major Beavis V.D., is posted to 247th W.R.F.A. Bde in General Artillery Orders. The men without Hats to-day. T-day Br. Mawson (attached to 4th Section DAC) G.S.W. in back. Rain continued then ceased.	
	30/16 /10			
	31/16 /10		Dry, clear day. Major Kidwell, O.C. 578th battery pays his first visit to the lines since joining the Brigade.	

[signature]

247 (York) Bde R.F.A. Vol 19

War Diary. November 1916

Lt Col M. Dickinson

49

B.E.F.

Army Form C. 2118

WAR DIARY
or
INTELLIGENCE SUMMARY
(Erase heading not required.)

Instructions regarding War Diaries and Intelligence Summaries are contained in F.S. Regs., Part II. and the Staff Manual respectively. Title Pages will be prepared in manuscript.

Place	Date	Hour	Summary of Events and Information	Remarks and references to Appendices
COURCELLES (LENS Sheet 11 1/10000)	1/11/16		Nothing of interest	
	2/11/16		" "	
	3/11/16		Z-day postponed until 7th inst. Instalment of 576th Battery Bdy Arty. trench to firing positions since joining J. Brigade.	
	4/11/16		Operations are interrupting preparations. Heavy rain at night.	
	5/11/16	3-8pm	Supplies, rations and issue after reorganisation. Arrival of the Base.	
	6/11/16	4-8pm	Rather highly weather. OC Brs attends Conference with regard to Operations and it is decided to proceed with them. On the 9th as Z-day situation happens but it is decided to stop on the slee line of the fighting is heavy.	
		6-8pm	Orders from at Conference are cancelled and operations apparently postponed.	JB

1875 Wt. W593/826 1,000,000 4/15 J.B.C. & A. A.D.S.S./Forms/C. 2118.

Army Form C. 2118

WAR DIARY
or
INTELLIGENCE SUMMARY
(Erase heading not required.)

Instructions regarding War Diaries and Intelligence Summaries are contained in F.S. Regs. Part II. and the Staff Manual respectively. Title Pages will be prepared in manuscript.

Place	Date	Hour	Summary of Events and Information	Remarks and references to Appendices
COURCELLES (Lens Sheet 11) 1/100000	7/11/16		Very heavy rain. Enemy shelling very active throughout day. Further earth slides in battle Headquarters.	
	8/11/16		Rain as heavy as ever. Situation an inevitably deferred and dumps are to be reduced. Bryan's battle Headquarters practically collapsed.	
	9/11/16		Serious day - brisk and clear. Considerable enemy airplane activity. Colonel rode over to GRENAS to inspect 578th Battery & lines of A, C, & D 241 Stations entered ORVILLE.	
	10/11/16		Cold day. Dull at times but no rain.	
	11/11/16		Showery day. Nothing of interest.	
	12/11/16		Go forward to Battle HQ at 3.0pm this being Y-day for the [illegible] Captn Scot Owen Comm and of B/165. 33rd Division	182/

WAR DIARY or INTELLIGENCE SUMMARY

Army Form C. 2118

Place	Date	Hour	Summary of Events and Information	Remarks and references to Appendices
K25&63. (HÉBUTERNE) 1/10000	13/11/16		Z-day. Two hrs. frightful fog. All batteries start off to time.	
		6.45 a.m.	Wear news of troops. Eastern exits of SERRE and trench and front runners of trenches in of Serre on the right and a few failures to feed but nothing serious.	
		7.15 a.m.		
		10.0 a.m.	About 20 prisoners are reached past the Aug-outs apparently from N.J. SERRE opposite 31st Division. Both Shells Northern and Southern Avenues heavily.	
	14/11/16	9.30 a.m.	Both Shell Railway Avenue with Gas Shells. Enemy artillery fairly active all day in Both areas. Enemy aeroplanes very daring but very active – three came over at an altitude of only about 500 feet.	
	15/11/16		Generic day but keen frost.	
	16/11/16		Keen frost and bitter wind.	

WAR DIARY or INTELLIGENCE SUMMARY

Army Form C. 2118

(Erase heading not required.)

Instructions regarding War Diaries and Intelligence Summaries are contained in F.S. Regs., Part II. and the Staff Manual respectively. Title Pages will be prepared in manuscript.

Place	Date	Hour	Summary of Events and Information	Remarks and references to Appendices
K.26.53. HEBUTERNE (1/10000)	17/11/16		Another keen frost. Capt. F.W. Buck. Awarded M.C. for gallantry on nights 21st–22nd July 1916 in extracting a wounded Field Gunner from the front line during heavy shell fire.	
	18/11/16	6-15 am	Thaw set in – cold weather – rainy day. Operations for capture of MUNICH & FRANKFORT trench on our right. No news as to success or failure.	
	19/11/16	2pm	Heavy artillery fire on 5th Divn. Enemy artillery fire continuously during early morning. Colonel E. Clifton V.D. here to take over command of Divisional Artillery during absence of General Key DSO on leave. Major Bevill 518th Batty assumes command D Bat during absence of Colonel Clifford.	JFC

1875 Wt. W593/826 1,000,000 4/15 J.B.C. & A. A.D.S.S./Forms/C. 2118.

Army Form C. 2118

WAR DIARY
or
INTELLIGENCE SUMMARY
(Erase heading not required.)

Instructions regarding War Diaries and Intelligence Summaries are contained in F. S. Regs., Part II. and the Staff Manual respectively. Title Pages will be prepared in manuscript.

Place	Date	Hour	Summary of Events and Information	Remarks and references to Appendices
COURCELLES (LENS II 1/10000)	19/11/16	4.0 pm	The Bar Hudsworth into COURCELLES except for shipments in duty at Battn Hq.	
	20/11/16		Battery commence to reduce Ammunition Dumps. 18/100 rounds per gun and was sent to 23rd and 42nd Div. Further 100 rounds per gun handed over	
	21/11/16			
	22/11/16		All remaining ammunition handed over and guns unharnessed to Bois-en-Artois	
			Brigade Hqrs. move back to Bois-en-Artois respen for the night. Brigade Hqrs. "A" "C" & "D" Batteries move into Gnl Army area. Area taken up.	
Bois-en-Artois	23/11/16		Humbercamps	
Humbercamps	24/11/16			

Hqrs
"A" Battery
518 Battery from and from General Humbercamps
"C" Battery
"D"

1875 Wt. W593/826 1,000,000 4/15 J.B.C. & A. A.D.S.S./Forms/C. 2118.

WAR DIARY or INTELLIGENCE SUMMARY

Army Form C. 2118

Place	Date	Hour	Summary of Events and Information	Remarks and references to Appendices
Number Camp	25/5/16		Brigade and Battery Commanders took over Battery positions and Headquarters in new area.	
	26/6		One Section from "A" "C" & "D" Batteries relieve corresponding Sections of Batteries of 4th, 75 & D. Batteries of 242 Bde R.F.A. 48th Div Arty. Major E.J. Birdwell, O.C. 518 Battery, admitted to Hospital and evacuated. Lieut L.J. Blake admitted to Hospital and evacuated. Major E.G. Clifford takes over Command of the Brigade.	
Bienvillers	27/6		Brigade Headquarters relieves Headquarters of 242nd Bde R.F.A. at Bienvillers. Remaining sections of "A" "C" Batteries complete relief. 1 Section from 518 Battery joins the Section of "D" Battery, and the other section relieved the section of 6914 Battery.	

WAR DIARY or INTELLIGENCE SUMMARY

Army Form C. 2118

Place	Date	Hour	Summary of Events and Information	Remarks and references to Appendices
Brenchley	7/16		Batteries take up positions as under:-	
Nr 55A			A Bty Bty. - E.8 d.5.2. + 1 gun at M.22.b.45/65 = Commanded by 2/Lt. J. Shuttleworth
N≡			B Bty - E.20.c.5.2 + E.n.d.55/50. Lt. A.N. Haynes
			D Bty - E.6.b.99/30 Lt. A.W. Holden
			516 Bty - E.8.d.1.1 Lt. Ainsford
			1 Cav. Div. Arty take over the line at 4 pm.	
			2/Lt Smith, 4 Cav Div. R.E's hand over Zero up and is attached to Bde. Hqrs.	
	26/4/16		516 Battery commence on Lection gun pits at E.8.c.6.1. Observation impossible. Unable to verify registration taken over from relieved Brigade.	
	22/4/16		— do —	

WAR DIARY
or
INTELLIGENCE SUMMARY

(Erase heading not required.)

Army Form C. 2118

Place	Date	Hour	Summary of Events and Information	Remarks and references to Appendices
Beauval	30/6		Observation impossible. Wagon lines of Hqrs. A, C and D Batteries move to ST AMAND. 518 Battery remain at HUMBERCAMP.	

J.F. Saunders Capt & Adjt
for O.C. 147 (W.R.) Bde R.F.A.

Staff Captain R.A.
    49th (W.R.) Division.

    ------------------,-------------

        Herewith copy of War Diary for transmission
to D.A.G. 3rd Echelon through usual channels, please.

                        H. Earnshaw Capt & Adjt
                    for Lieut. Colonel. V.D., R.F.A.
        Commanding 247th (W.R.) Brigade R.F.A.(T).

2/11/1916.

Vol 20

SECRET.

WAR DIARY.

OF

247th (W) Brigade R.F.A.

FOR

December 1916.

2nd Gloucesters Bttn R.F.A.

War Diary ~ Dec. 1916

49th Div.

WAR DIARY
or
INTELLIGENCE SUMMARY
(Erase heading not required.)

Army Form C. 2118

Instructions regarding War Diaries and Intelligence Summaries are contained in F. S. Regs., Part II. and the Staff Manual respectively. Title Pages will be prepared in manuscript.

Place	Date	Hour	Summary of Events and Information	Remarks and references to Appendices
Brenellos -sur-Bois	1/12/16		'A' Btry Bakery registered B18 & I.9.	
		11.10 pm	Area round 'A' Btry Bakery shelled by 77 mm, 4.2 & gas shells.	
"	2/12/16		Very quiet day.	
	3/12/16		General shrapnel C.B. DSO. nicks round Bakery Position. Very quiet day.	
		7.30 pm	'A' Bakery fire 186 rounds in conjunction with French Mortars and Machine Guns of 9th Division on C.11.5.6 - C.5d. 35/20 - CHEMIN des DAMES. The object was to induce the enemy to man his parapets in force, and then to enfilade his trenches with M.Gs. & 18 prs.	
"	4/12/16	11.21 am	'A' Btry Bakery R.F.A. fire on aerodrome Post call E.13d 2.3.	S.A.

Army Form C. 2118

WAR DIARY
or
INTELLIGENCE SUMMARY
(Erase heading not required.)

Instructions regarding War Diaries and Intelligence Summaries are contained in F.S. Regs., Part II and the Staff Manual respectively. Title Pages will be prepared in manuscript.

Place	Date	Hour	Summary of Events and Information	Remarks and references to Appendices
BIENVILLERS AU-BOIS	5/4/16	12.40 pm — 8pm	The Battery occupied by A/242 Battery at 88 b 5 1. was subjected to heavy hostile shelling. At 12.40pm the Battery was registered by aeroplane and intermittent shelling with 5.9's; 4.2's; 4.2's; and lachrymatory shells then took place until 8.0pm. Over 200 rounds in all were fired. Two direct hits were obtained upon gun pits, one shell penetrating No 1 Gun emplacement and putting the gun out of action. The shelling was directed by aeroplane and chiefly confined to the Right Section. 3 men gassed & 1 man slightly wounded. Lieut E de Se Drew of 246 Brigade was ordered to take temporary command of B/242 Battery (Capt 518 Battery)	

1875 Wt. W593/326 1,000,000 4/15 J.B.C. & A. A.D.S.S./Forms/C. 2118.

Army Form C. 2118

WAR DIARY
or
INTELLIGENCE SUMMARY

(Erase heading not required.)

Instructions regarding War Diaries and Intelligence Summaries are contained in F.S. Regs., Part II. and the Staff Manual respectively. Title Pages will be prepared in manuscript.

Place	Date	Hour	Summary of Events and Information	Remarks and references to Appendices
Benvillers au-bois	5/12/16		Very quiet day. To-day there was an anti-aircraft course released by the 138th Infantry Brigade of the 46th Division to take. The 46th Infantry Brigade of the 46th Division to be taken released by the 138th Brigade of 46th Division. Division having taken over the line from the 46th Division.	
	6/12/16			
	7/12/16	10.0 am	The portion of 6 & 9 3 (D's 44) was subjected to hostile shelling with about 80 rs. H. shells. One shell penetrated cookhouse but no casualties were sustained. Owing to Capt D. Known not having returned from leave, Major Clifford was unable to proceed to the Artillery Course at Wedcliffe, which takes place on the 10th Dec. 1916.	

1875 Wt. W593/826 1,000,000 4/15 J.B.C. & A. A.D.S.S./Forms/C. 2118.

WAR DIARY or INTELLIGENCE SUMMARY

Army Form C. 2118

Place	Date	Hour	Summary of Events and Information	Remarks and references to Appendices
Keruglen an Bail	8/7/16		G.O.C. called at Group Hqrs. very wet day. The Hy Arty of HQ Div Arty came up into position in rear of our Hqrs. for Special Operations.	
	9th		Brig. Gen. Ross Johnson R.A. Corps made round positions of "A" and "B" Hvy Batteries. Again very wet day. – Very little fire on either side.	
	10/7/16		Capt F. Ellicoop is ordered to report to New Hqrs. at 6 Bae. and take over command of B Hvy Battery. Information having been received that the 3rd Bn. Yorks. will relieve the Bn. on Sector 61 A1.9 – Reconnaissance of Honky road. Orders carried out a conversation-bombardment on that part of the enemy front. a scheme being agreed to in conjunction with G.O.C. 138th Inf. Bde.	

WAR DIARY
or
INTELLIGENCE SUMMARY

(Erase heading not required.)

Army Form C. 2118

Instructions regarding War Diaries and Intelligence Summaries are contained in F.S. Regs., Part II. and the Staff Manual respectively. Title Pages will be prepared in manuscript.

Place	Date	Hour	Summary of Events and Information	Remarks and references to Appendices
Beuvry au-bois	10/12/16		Beuvry in retaliation for our fire. The enemy heavily shelled Beuvry at 9.27 pm for a period of about 10 minutes.	
	11/12/16		Enemy Parry Rang Gun came out Bombardments of Chemin des Dames, where double Trench Mortars are supposed to be.	
	12/12/16		About? Parry fire 50 rounds on 630 a 0 3 to 3 19 0 0 where considerable movement is reported. Lt. Col. G Clifford returns from leave and takes over Command of the Brigade, from Major E.b Clifford.	
		8.50pm	Beuvry shelled.	
	13/12/16		A concentrated bombardment to damage the enemy's works in the Manky Salient to take place from 11 am. Horry and Rost have orders to fire 600 rounds each into Manky	

1875 Wt. W593/826 1,000,000 4/15 J.B.C. & A. A.D.S.S./Forms/C. 2118.

WAR DIARY
or
INTELLIGENCE SUMMARY

Army Form C. 2118

Place	Date	Hour	Summary of Events and Information	Remarks and references to Appendices
Beaumetz sur-Oise	13/12/16		The object of the bombardment was to force the enemy to concentrate his labour on the front lines instead of working on his rear lines	
	14/12/16	4.5pm	Enemy Shells Bienvillers with about 50. 4.25	
		6.50pm	Infantry Brigade call for "TEST Y.2." Owing to the screens being up in front of the guns, 5 minutes elapsed before a fire was opened	
	15/12/16		Very quiet all day. Sent G HBs returns from Corps	
	16/12/16		Very quiet day. Capt Saunders Sn'd to Ave. Bad visibility. Took would not to have a quiet day	
	17/12/16		Another quiet day. Rain coming now. Post so an E most into (Training) Area on 25th. Y.21.51. the 46th DA taking our front	
	18/12/16		Retring Letter of G/241 attached to Eighth Corps for a raid on the [?]	

WAR DIARY
or
INTELLIGENCE SUMMARY

Army Form C. 2118

Place	Date	Hour	Summary of Events and Information	Remarks and references to Appendices
BIENVILLERS	18/12/16		GOMMECOURT Salient. Battery Commanders and Bryan Commander of 232(NM) F.A.Bde reconnoitred their positions.	
	19/12/16	5.30 pm	Quiet day. Kern shot - quiet day. Few rounds on enemy's back areas.	
	20/12/16	9.30 am 10.0 am	One bright day - Enemies retaliating fire on our front. Short concentrated bombardment on a battery position. We claim a M.E.4 t 65-20. Wired to retreat to be actors to 19th Bnd.	
			A/247 30 rounds	
			B/247 20 "	
			D/247 60 "	
	21/12/16	12 noon 2.4 pm	Heavy rain from 10.0 am until 12.0 noon. Stand for command of Centre Group to 232nd Bn RFA (T). March from BIENVILLERS	

WAR DIARY or INTELLIGENCE SUMMARY

Army Form C. 2118

(Erase heading not required.)

Instructions regarding War Diaries and Intelligence Summaries are contained in F. S. Regs., Part II. and the Staff Manual respectively. Title Pages will be prepared in manuscript.

Place	Date	Hour	Summary of Events and Information	Remarks and references to Appendices
GROUCHES (LENS 11 1/100,000)	21/12/16		Section march independently to billets in GROUCHES; the Col. & one marching in at 7.30 pm. Two Coms. help to move trucks. Three standings an Ben. especially three of 'D' Battery in Bois de Pret.	
	22/12/16		Men' billets an fair & Officers' horses. Blustering wind and latter turns into drizzle. Bryan and Major Phipps. Colonel and	
	23/12/16		Survived ho. O.P. Bde Gee round Batteries in afternoon. Selected O.P. upon billets, standings etc.	
	24/12/16		O.C. Bde has a Conference with Battery Commanders to the question of general discipline & plans for training billets in Riel Ores	

Army Form C. 2118

WAR DIARY
or
INTELLIGENCE SUMMARY

(Erase heading not required.)

Instructions regarding War Diaries and Intelligence Summaries are contained in F. S. Regs., Part II. and the Staff Manual respectively. Title Pages will be prepared in manuscript.

Place	Date	Hour	Summary of Events and Information	Remarks and references to Appendices
GROUCHES	24/12		General clean up & preparation for Xmas Day.	
(LENS II) (YPRES)	25/12	9.30 am	Church Parade. Holy Communion.	
		10 a.m	During the morning 75 hours from each of 'B' & 'C' batteries were sent to Lt Gens Tison & for "dipping". The G.O.C. Division & G.O.C. R.A. called on the Brigade to express their good wishes for Xmas & the New Year. 'A' & 'D' batteries have their Xmas dinner. Good feeds & we have a few light showers rain. Headquarters, 'C', & 'B' batteries have their Xmas dinners.	
	26/12		Nothing of interest.	
	27/12			
	28/12	9.00 am	'B' battery marches under command of Lt POLDEN to be attached to 35th Divisional Artillery, 9 am billeted in WANQUETIN. 1 Gun of suspected range on 'C' battery is sent to Woolwich.	

WAR DIARY
or
INTELLIGENCE SUMMARY

Army Form C. 2118

Place	Date	Hour	Summary of Events and Information	Remarks and references to Appendices
GRAUCHES (LENS H) (1/10000)	29/16 12		O.C. Bde inspected "A", "C", & "D" Batteries & H.Q. horse lines, (am parks), & billets. Frost broken & we have continuous rain.	
	3/16 12	10.00am	G.O.C. R.A. inspected Bryan lines, billets and horses. He inspected the personnel. An dismounted parade and delivered a short address to the Brigade during which Sonnne offensive.	
		2.30am		
	3/16 12	9.30am	Dawn an march for the Divisional Artillery by which the Brigade is divided up between the Divisions of the Army.	
			Church Parade.	

Andrew Stubbs
Lt Col. Comdg (late) R.F.A. Bde.

O.C. A/247 Battery.
    B/247 ..   (for information)
    C/247 ..
    D/247 ..

Following telegram from 46th Division begins :-
Intelligence has been received that the 3rd Battalion 77th Regiment will this evening relieve the 1st Battalion in Sector E 18 a 1.9 to HANNESCAMPS - MONCHY ROAD AAA Brigadier Y Sector should arrange with his Group Commander for bursts of Artillery fire and should see that machine gun fire is arranged for AAA The roads used for relief are from BUCQUOY to QUARRY F 7 a 5.3 thence via MONCHY GRABEN - KREUZ GRABEN - and LANDWEHR GRABEN AAA Message ends.

In consequence of the above the following Artillery Programme will be carried out tonight.

Battery.	Time.	Objective.	Ammunition.
		PHASE I.	
A/247. (2 guns)	7.5.p.m. - 7.7.p.m.	Search C.T's from E 12 b 35/40 to junction of trenches F 7 a 00/56.	3 rounds per gun per minute. A.X.
(2 guns)	-do-	E 12 b 5.1 - F 7 a 3.3.	-do-
C/247.	-do-	C.T. E 12 b 5.1 - E 12 c 90/16 LANDWEHR GRABEN.	-do-
D/247.	-do-	Strong points :- E 12 c 35/40. E 12 a 50/15. E 12 a 25/90. F 7 a 00/56.	1 round per gun per minute.
		PHASE II.	
A/247. C/247.	9.15 - 9.17.p.m.	Repeat PHASE I.	Rate of fire as for PHASE I.
D/247.	-do-	E 12 c 35/40. E 12 a 50/15 E 11 b 99/00 E 5 d 80/00.	1 round per gun per minute.
		PHASE III.	
A/247. C/247.	10.35 - 10.37.p.m.	Repeat PHASE I.	As for Phase I.
D/247.	-do-	Repeat PHASE II.	As for Phase II.

Between PHASES 1 and 2 and 2 and 3, <u>D/247 Battery</u> will fire occasional rounds on Company Headquarters at E 12 c 35/40 - E 12 a 50/15.
Ammunition allotted - 26 rounds.
Watches will be synchronised at 6.30.p.m.

10/12/1916.

                            Captain & Adjutant,
                            247th (W.R.) Bde R.F.A.

S E C R E T.

49th Divisional Artillery Order No. 45.

Reference Maps RANSART &
FONQUEVILLERS, 1/10,000.

9th December 1916.

1. A Bombardment of the MONCHY SALIENT will take place about December 13th 1916.

   Zero hour will be notified later.

   The action of the 49th Divisional Artillery will be as on the attached tables.

2. The object of the Bombardment is to damage the enemy's works in the MONCHY SALIENT and force him to concentrate his labour there, instead of working on his rear lines.

3. Registration will be carried out on December 10th and succeeding days. No rounds will be fired into MONCHY Village during registration.

4. Attached batteries will probably leave this area on the evening of December 13th or immediately after the bombardment.

5. Detailed instructions as to the dumping of ammunition have been issued separately.

   Ammunition should be kept as far as possible boxed until required.

6. Watches will be synchronised at 9.0.a.m. on December 13th.

7. ACKNOWLEDGE.

(sd) E. J. SKINNER, Major R.A.
Brigade Major R.A. 49th (W.R.) Div.

--- 2 ---

O.C. A/247 Battery
     B/247 ..
     C/247 ..
     D/247 ..

Forwarded for your information.

Earnshaw Captain R.F.A.
Adjutant
247th (W.R.) Brigade R.F.A.

9/12/1916.

O.C. A/247 Battery.
    B/247 ..
    C/247 ..
    D/247 ..

AMMUNITION INSTRUCTIONS FOR FORTHCOMING OPERATIONS.

1. Ammunition is allotted to Batteries as follows.

    A/247)
    C/247) to be notified later.

    B/247.   660 rounds BX.
    D/247.   660 rounds BX.

2. The D.A.C. will complete these dumps by the night of 11-12th.December.

3. All Ammunition will be conveyed to the Gun positions and dumped boxed.

4. All boxes will be taken on charge and returned with cases on completion of operations.

5. This allotment of Ammunition is in addition to and distinct from any ammunition at present on charge of batteries.

                                        Captain R.F.A.
                                        Adjutant,
                       247th (W.R.) Brigade R.F.A.

9/12/1916.

S E C R E T.

T A S K S.
- - - -

D/247 Battery R.F.A.

Code.	Time.	Objective.	Remarks.
B.3.	0.0. - 60.	PHASE I. Bombard front Line E 5 a 40/00 - E 5 a 15/35.	Steady rate of fire 1 round per gun per minute.
	60 - 70.	PHASE II. As in Phase I	
C.4	70 - 140.	PHASE III. E 5 a 60/05 - E 5 a 40/40	
	140 - 150.	PHASE IV. As in Phase II.	
	150 - 200.	PHASE V. As in Phase I.	

RATES OF FIRE WHERE NOT OTHERWISE SPECIFIED - 4.5" How. 1 round per gun per min.

B/247 Battery R.F.A.

Code.	Time.	Objective.	Remarks.
B.2.	0.0. - 60.	PHASE I. Bombard front line E 5 a 15/35 - W 29 c 15/20.	Steady rate of fire 1 round per gun per minute.
	60 - 70.	PHASE II. As in Phase I.	
C.3.	70 - 140.	PHASE III. E 5 a 40/40 - W 29 c 35/05.	
	140 - 150.	PHASE IV. As in Phase II.	
	150 - 200.	PHASE V. As in Phase I.	

RATES OF FIRE WHERE NOT OTHERWISE SPECIFIED - 4.5" How. 1 round per gun per minute.

24th M.O.F.A. Ste

Cuba

Soc 21

49

War Diary – January 1919.

WAR DIARY or INTELLIGENCE SUMMARY

Army Form C. 2118

Place	Date	Hour	Summary of Events and Information	Remarks and references to Appendices
GROUCHES (LENS II) /10000	1/7/17		In accordance with the Reorganisation Scheme all details for the transfer of one Section of D/247 to D/245 and one Section to D/246 are got out and into of Surplus personnel, horses, and equipment prepared. Also details in connection with the further reorganisation of Artillery in the Army and the transfer of 1 A/247 into the Section of D/247 to 503 Bde and C/247 with one Section of D/247 to the 232nd Bde or further took on in connection with the reorganisation.	
	2/7/17			
	3/7/17	11.0 am	C/247 today Command of Lt. - Temporary Major. K. Strom with Lt. Blake & Lt. Brunton, of 225 Bvt. Harvey march out of Grouches to report to 232nd Bde. Lt. - acting Capt. - Haynes, A.A. to Captain of the Battery and one G. Nyort to them on his return from leave. 2nd Lt. J.R. Horton also on leave will take the place of Nothing the roll. The report to H.Q. 49th D.A.	

WAR DIARY
or
INTELLIGENCE SUMMARY
(Erase heading not required.)

Army Form C. 2118

Place	Date	Hour	Summary of Events and Information	Remarks and references to Appendices
GROUCHES (LENS II 1/100000 and FRANCE Sheet 51C 1/40000)	3/7/17	11.10 am	Lt. Colonel C. Clifford V.D. rode with Major Strover M.C. to LUCHEUX where they were met by Br. General Kay DSO, CRA. who rode with them. Major General E.M. Percival C.B., D.S.O. G.O.C. Division took the Salute at T.17.a.7.9. And then riding on to the head of the Column, halted it and calling out the officers and NCOs addressed a short address saying how he appreciated the note which had been sent by the battery and how he was certain that they would always give a good account of themselves. D/247 left Seton under the Command of Lt Boden & GROUCHES to report to 232nd Bde but were unfortunately too late to follow in after C. battery to the march past.	
	4/7/17	11.0 am	A/247 battery with Capt Emery in Command and Lt Armitage MC and Lt Stevens marched out to report to	SF

WAR DIARY
or
INTELLIGENCE SUMMARY

Army Form C. 2118

Place	Date	Hour	Summary of Events and Information	Remarks and references to Appendices
GROUCHES. LENS II 1/10000	4/17		150th Brigade. Major E.G. Clifford was on leave in England as also was Lt.Col. Shuttleworth. Yesterday 13/247 Regiment with B/247 was reported with the addition that 13/247 marching at of Grouches at 11-10 am was in time to follow or to use of B/247. In the meanwhile poor; Lt. G.T. Gorman Commanded this section to be relieved by Lt. A.N. Pitten on his return from VI Corps area where he had gone in command of B/247 to take part in some Manoeuvres.	
	5/17		Capt. J.H. Lewis M.C. relieved Lt.A.N. Pitten in Command of B/247	
	6/17		Nothing.	
	7/17	3-0pm	B/247 under Command of Capt. Lewis M.C. and Lt. Lord, Bell Barlow and 2nd Lt. Chippendale returned from VI Corps area and went into billets at BOUT-DES-PRÉS.	
	8/17		1st Section B/247 marched out to form D/245 Battery and Staff Capt. J.H. Eddison M.C. to proceed Capt. J.H. Eddison	

WAR DIARY
INTELLIGENCE SUMMARY

Army Form C. 2118

Place	Date	Hour	Summary of Events and Information	Remarks and references to Appendices
GROOTEBEKE (I-ENS II 1/10 m)	8/17		The Senior Officers of the Brigade now consist of:—	

Brigade H.Q.
- Lt-Colonel C. Clapton V.D.
- Capt J.E. Faudrew M.C. — Adjutant
- Capt R.V. Facell R.A.M.C. (T) — M.O. i/c
- Capt F.G. Bunton A.V.C. — V.O. i/c
- Lt J. Help — Messing Officer
- Lt J.C.J. Goodman — in charge of Ft Section DAC with 150th Bde
- Lt A.W. Bell — posted to D.A.C.
- Lt V.G. Baden
- Lt R.G. Lord
- Lt S. Hurry
- 2Lt A.J. Cumming — posted to D.A.C.
- Lt R.S. Eccles — at Course of Signalling at BARLY
- Lt Chippendale — on Course at 3rd Army Signal Mothers

The Brigade HQ is being kept in cost watches awaiting further plans.

S.H.

WAR DIARY or INTELLIGENCE SUMMARY

Army Form C. 2118

Place	Date	Hour	Summary of Events and Information	Remarks and references to Appendices
GROUCHES.	9/17.		Nothing doing.	
(LENS II / HUDSON)	10/17		Nothing doing	
	4/17		"	
	12/17		} Matters of Interest.	
	13/17			
	23/17		M Portillo, Interpreter of Bdr., been to report to 245th Bde CRA	
	24/17		Capt RY Searle RAM.C.(T) twero Bde to report to DD.M.S.	
	25/17		XVIII Corps for duty.	
	26/17 To 31/17		} Nothing doing.	

LIEUTENANT COLONEL V.D., R.F.A
247th. (W.R.) BRIGADE R.F.A.

Army Form C. 2118

WAR DIARY
or
INTELLIGENCE SUMMARY
(Erase heading not required.)

Instructions regarding War Diaries and Intelligence Summaries are contained in F.S. Regs., Part II. and the Staff Manual respectively. Title Pages will be prepared in manuscript.

Place	Date	Hour	Summary of Events and Information	Remarks and references to Appendices
GROUCHES	1/2/17 to 25/2/17		Details of 'B' and 'D' batteries and Headquarters of B'de remain in billets awaiting news as to departure.	
	26/2/17		Orders arrive for departure of all that remains of 247th (mre) Bde. Lt. C. Clifford VD. RFA(T) and the Adjutant, Capt J.E. Earnshaw MC. RFA are to proceed to England and report at WOOLWICH with guns to, taking over an Army Issue Artillery Brigade. Lt. F.G. Stops RFA(T), Orderly Officer, to report to 58th Divisional Artillery for duty. B.S.M. Foster to return to England with Lt. Col. C. Clifford as Adjutant. All men & N.C.Os. of Bde Hq. & details to be attached to 49th Divisional Artillery.	
	27/2/17		Went in connection with above.	
	28/2/17	7.0am	Details march out to join 49th D.A.	

J.E. Earnshaw
Capt
27/2/17 (MC)RFA(T) Adjt.

49TH DIVISION

247TH BRIGADE R.F.A.

MAY 1915-FEB 1917

BDE BROKEN UP

49TH DIVISION

47

2nd 7th (W.R.) Bde R.F.A.
late 1/3 WR Bde   K.E 13

War Diary - May 1916

+9" (W.R.) Duncan

Army Form C. 2118

WAR DIARY
or
INTELLIGENCE SUMMARY
(Erase heading not required.)

Instructions regarding War Diaries and Intelligence Summaries are contained in F. S. Regs., Part II. and the Staff Manual respectively. Title Pages will be prepared in manuscript.

Place	Date	Hour	Summary of Events and Information	Remarks and references to Appendices
BERTEAU-COURT	1/5/16.		Reveille Rather for Bryant at 5-30 A.M.	
	2/5/16.	6.0 pm	Party of Officers W.O.s and men paraded at Bn. H.Q. for purpose of proceeding to ABBEVILLE in order to draw Guns, horses, harness and draught animals for D.3. Battery.	
	3/5/16		Parade Roll G.O.R.A. Division for 7th Battery with Staff Captain, 6 n.c.o.s Officers and 20 N.C.O.s horses & gun with Officers below in the attendance of the F.O.O. arrived at Major Steven (O.R.A.) Farm for Situation of the F.O.O. Ammunition Column hands over to him in exchange for motor transport by D.3.	
	4/5/16.		Methods of instruct.	
	5/5/16.		Bn. Rosa March.	
	6/5/16.	2.30 pm	Inf. & Bn. Signallers	
	7/5/16.	9.30 p.m	Front Service at Bn. H.Q.	
	8/5/16.		Miniature Range sel up for use of Bn. all ranks of Manoeuvring for C. Offrs. N.C.Os.' Staff course for 75 and D.3. Gun drill, shelter work and Signalling on Companies	

Army Form C. 2118

WAR DIARY
or
INTELLIGENCE SUMMARY

(Erase heading not required.)

Instructions regarding War Diaries and Intelligence Summaries are contained in F. S. Regs., Part II. and the Staff Manual respectively. Title Pages will be prepared in manuscript.

Place	Date	Hour	Summary of Events and Information	Remarks and references to Appendices
BERTEAU-COURT	9/5/16	8.30 AM	Brigade staff together with English Battery staff and Jun and F.O.W. of 7th & 8th & 9th Batteries met General Hay (R.A.) and spent the morning up to 1 p.m. practicing coming into action and going out "Come of fire".	
	10/5/16		All intrum Still Bar + Manoeuvring	
	11/5/16		Practice Artillery Brigade served at into of 17th Battery. 7th & D3 did a "dual van" with Colonel tolens up positions, going out "Come of fire" etc.	
	12/5/16		8th & 9th Batteries practice taking up positions & going into action of fire under shell.	
	13/5/16		Boys & cancer in all units. This am Artillery Board & General Cur re-numbered and sent to future reference no 24 & (N.P.) 13 M.	
	14/5/16	2.30 PM	Staff Commpunications exercise this p.m. at Hangard tube Too set. Officers return up to Regn line at Vauxerrues & do anything.	
	15/5/16		Early service. & Jun SM & Signallers plus Frenfred. Exchange of shows with 9th Ammunition Column.	

WAR DIARY
or
INTELLIGENCE SUMMARY

Army Form C. 2118

Place	Date	Hour	Summary of Events and Information	Remarks and references to Appendices
BERTEN-COURT	17/5/16		1st day of General Stand Down. Orders for 6-horse teams. Only A and C and 1 Firs & Res & Ammn. Col. and C. O. Y.C. Battery.	
	18/5/16		2nd day of Stand down & transferred to W/leg. T.M. Battery. General Stand down. Ammn. Col. on fatigues for clearing from B.A.C. Battery to Bde. 2nd Stage. Ammn. Col. all fats disposed.	
	19/5/16		Route March for 'B' and 'D' Batteries.	
	20/5/16		D.S. carried out for an Howitzer Battery coming into action on its own — both the Followers and the Battery to be instructed on account of German methods.	
	21/5/16		Bde. H.Q. Staff also Communication Scheme in morning. Horse Service at Bde. Headquarters after which Capt. Stanley gave the H.O. Y.C. Bde. Staff a lecture on "Sanitation" to Officers and N.C.O.s	
	22/5/16		A & C Batteries have a Route March in the am. B Battery the Battery Drill. D Battery Gunnery Drill.	
		2.30pm	Divine Service for all Officers	

WAR DIARY or INTELLIGENCE SUMMARY

Army Form C. 2118

(Erase heading not required.)

Instructions regarding War Diaries and Intelligence Summaries are contained in F.S. Regs., Part II. and the Staff Manual respectively. Title Pages will be prepared in manuscript.

Place	Date	Hour	Summary of Events and Information	Remarks and references to Appendices
BERTEAU-COURT	23/5/16	8-30AM	Headquarters – Signallers A & C Batteries – Burry Drill. B Battery – Sing Exercise D at Aylward of O.C.	
		2-240 2-45 to 3-30pm	Munition Range C /3 / Battery Officers and NCO's Officers of A.C. & D batteries under Lt. Warden.	
	24/5/16	8-30AM	Headquarters – Signalling A & C. Batteries – Sun Drill and Laying B: Battery – Byd Drill with Firing Battery. D: Battery – Burry Drill with Limbers.	
		2-0 to 3-0pm	Munition Range for Officers and NCO's of all units.	
		5-30pm	Officers Signalling.	
	25/5/16	8-30 AM	Headquarters – Signallers A & C Batteries – Burry Drill. B: Burry Exercise & Battery Stop Exercise. D: At Aylward of O.C.	G.W.
		2-0 to 3-0pm	Munition Range for Officers and NCO's of all units	
		5-30 to 6-30pm	Officers Signalling	

1875 Wt. W593/826 1,000,000 4/15 J.B.C. & A. A.D.S.S./Forms/C. 2118.

WAR DIARY
or
INTELLIGENCE SUMMARY
(Erase heading not required.)

Army Form C. 2118

Instructions regarding War Diaries and Intelligence Summaries are contained in F. S. Regs., Part II. and the Staff Manual respectively. Title Pages will be prepared in manuscript.

Place	Date	Hour	Summary of Events and Information	Remarks and references to Appendices
	26/6		Training of Officers and men of D.A.C. in Gun Drill both 18 lb & Howitzer Ammunition.	
		8.30a	"B" Battery Still Gun Parade with 2 nd 60th F.A.Bde.	
			A.C.L.D. Entries - Gun Lecture.	
		3-4pm	Ch: Adj: & Orderly Officer go to a scheme with G.O.C. Evreux, G.O.C. R.A. Divison, G.O.C. Infantry to our Stations	
			at VALHEUREUX.	
	27/6	6.30a	"A"&"B" Batteries — at disposal of O's L.	
			"C" Battery — Driving Drill.	
			"D" Battery — at disposal of O.L.	
		2 to 4pm	Cleaning -up.	
	28/6		Church Parade.	
			Inspection of "B""D"&"D" Bakery which has been reported at Canopho owing to German Morale Jams up Dispatch Rep.	
			Lieut G. J. Emerson posted to "C" Bakery. 2t Bakery. 2t K. Chipperdale to "B" Bakery 2t D.L. Measures to "A" Bakery	

WAR DIARY
or
INTELLIGENCE SUMMARY
(Erase heading not required.)

Army Form C. 2118

Place	Date	Hour	Summary of Events and Information	Remarks and references to Appendices
	29/5/16	9.30 a.m.	Sections "A" & "C" Batteries - Gas Exercise. "B" Battery - Shell order - Firing Battery with Battery Staff. Sections of "D" Battery - Firing drill.	
		2.30 p.m.	Miniature Range for Officers N.Co's of "D" Battery	
	30/5/16	8.45 a.m.	Remainder of Brigade - less B/247 Battery - proceed to join up Sections at VARENNES. Route - Talmas - Rubeville - Fontenoint - Harponville - Varennes.	
			Headquarters proceed to ENGLEBELMER and are attached to 9th H.A.G. NORTHERN COUNTER BATTERY GROUP.	
			B/247 Battery attached to 248 (NR) Bde R.F.A for discipline and administration.	
	31/5/16		Brigade with 10" Corps HA for administration.	

J.E. Earnshaw Lt Col. RFA

Lieutenant Colonel V.D.R.F.A.
Commdg. 247 (West Rid). Bde. R.F.A

49th Divisional Artillery.

247th BRIGADE.

ROYAL FIELD ARTILLERY.

JUNE 1916

Place	Date	Hour	Summary of Events and Information	Remarks and references to Appendices
Engelbelmer	1/12/16		Headquarters of Brigade Established at Q.25.a.5.8. (ref 57d S.E 1/20,000) Batteries occupy positions as under.	
			Battery — Position — Reference — Arc	
			A/247 (18pr) — 60 — Q.22.d 18/52 — 45° – 120° } Ref Sheet 57d (1/20,000)	
			B/247 (18pr) — 84 — Q.22.c 52/02 — 35° – 115°	
			D/247 (4.5") — 78 — Q.34.c 4.8 — 30° – 100°	
	2/12/16	5.50am	C/247 Battery fires on Q.15.b & 25.30.	
	3/12/16	10am	B/247 Battery fired 49 rounds H.E. and 18 L on registration	
		12.30pm	and calibration of guns on Q.19.c.1.5 and Q.24.d 45.85	
		6.30pm	A/247 Battery fires 30 rounds A on Q.19 & 89/90 and Q.7c7/45 on registration	
			Battery Honors Gazette Published	
			Lee of 4/5 S.E Enriched awarded Military Cross	
			The nominations awarded Military Medal	
			1073 Gr. A.T. Pelcut } A/247 Battery	
			1511 Dr. J. McManur }	
			1051 Gr. J. White } C/247 Battery	
			1467 . J. W. Hall }	

Place	Date	Hour	Summary of Events and Information	Remarks and references to Appendices
Englebelmer	4/6	12.20 am to 1.20 am	A/247 Battery fired 100 rounds A and AX fire on Target 34 by order of Counter Battery Group.	
			A/247 Battery. Registered d.25.c.99.75; d.25.c.75.60; d.25.c.9.5; d.25.d.1.2; d.25.8.4.5; d.21.6.9.9.	
		9% 9.15pm } 10.5% 10.20pm }	D. Bty Battery:- Fired 6 rounds on new trench from Q.12.6.0 to 80/95	
	5/6	12.45% 12.55am 1.50% 2.0am }	Further 6 rounds fired on above.	
		6.30pm	A/247 Battery fired 6 rounds on d.19 & 89.90 in checking registration and correct.	
		11% 11.30pm }	A Battery Fired 60 rounds on targets "51" to "63" inclusive, and 40 rounds on target 47 as per operation orders attached. B Battery fired 40 rounds on target 62. Vide operation orders attached.	1.

Place	Date	Hour	Summary of Events and Information	Remarks and references to Appendices
Englebelmer	5/6	11% to 11.50 pm	B/247 Battery fired in conjunction with 32nd and 33rd Divisional Artillery, made Operation Orders attached. 25 rounds at Support trench in Q21 & 25 rounds on trench in Q22 & and 25 rounds on R25 a 92.00 to R25 d 10.92. 25 rounds on R25 c 99.97 to R25 d 00.75.	
	6/6/16	5.10 to 5.20 pm	B/247 Battery fired 10 rounds on hostile battery at R15 c 5.3	
	7/9/16	11.20 am	B/247 Battery fired 20 rounds on Working Party at R20 a 62/59.	
	8/6/16		Ammunition Dump marked at VARENNES	
	9/6/16		B/247 Battery. All four guns in action. 7.15 pm fired 5 rounds on R19 d 90/65 in registration.	

Place	Date	Hour	Summary of Events and Information	Remarks and references to Appendices
Englebelmer	10/6	11.57pm	A/247 Battery fired 10 rounds on target 40 at request of Counter Battery Group.	
		3.45pm	A/247 Battery. 10 rounds fired on Target 40 at request of Counter Battery Group.	
		8.45pm	B/247 Battery fired 10 rounds and A/15 = 60/12 to R21 a 59/62	
		11.30pm	— fired 11 rounds at targets 81 at request of Counter Battery Group.	
	11/6	12.12am	A/247 Battery fired 20 rounds on targets 51/6 65 inclusive at request of Counter Battery Group.	
	12/6		all quiet	
	13/6 19/6	2.58pm	Summary returned on CHARLES AVENUE.	
	19/6	12.19pm	B/247 Battery fired 12 rounds from R20 a 31/40 to R20 c 37/96 in accordance with Counter Battery Group's instruction	

Place	Date	Hour	Summary of Events and Information	Remarks and references to Appendices
Engelbelmer	15/6	8.15 pm	A/241 Battery fired 14 rounds on working party at R.33.d.1.9 by order of Cauleux Battery Group.	
		8.35 pm	6/241 Battery fired 13 rounds on target 62 by order of Cauleux Battery Group. (R.20 a.58 48)	
	16/6	9.45% to 11.30 am	D Battery fired 45 rounds on Q.24.d 45/80; Q.24 d 5.8 R.13 d 7.8; R.20 c 6.3; and R.7 c 2.5 London Gazette published following following Officers and NCO's of the Brigade "Mentioned in Despatches" Lieut Col. C. Clifford Capt J. Killick No "7" Dvr. J. R. Bracken No "49" Dr. 1436 Bomb. N. W. Bricley N. Driver	
	17/6	10 am to 12 noon	D Battery fired 19 rounds on R.15 a 8.6 - Registration by aeroplane.	

Place	Date	Hour	Summary of Events and Information	references to Appendices
Englebelmer 18a6	18/6	10am	D. Battery fired 45 rounds on Q.24 & 45/80, Q.19c Q.19c 09/55.	
		11.20 am	Q.19c 15/30 & Q.13 d 86 in checking registration and harassing of Charges.	
		6.30 pm	- do - Fired OK along enemy's front line trenches in Q.19 and R.25 to silence hostile rifle fire at our aeroplane.	
	19/6		All quiet	
	20/6	9.20 am	D. Battery fired 6 rounds at enemy's Battery R.8 & 99/52.	
		11.20		
		12 m.	Fired 9 rounds on Q.19c 1.6 & Q.13 d 75.80 in registration.	
			16 rounds at Q.8a Bois d'Hollande in confirming various propellants, the result of which was not very satisfactory.	
		7.30 pm	"C"Battery. Fired 21 rounds on Q.19 & 19/70 Crucifix - Bois d'Hollande in registration and calibration	

Place	Date	Hour	Summary of Events and Information	references to Appendices
Englebermer	20/9	1.20 to 1.35 pm	"A" Battery. 12 rounds fired on d.8 & 93/52 and d.8 & 97.48 at request of Camden Battery Group.	
	21/9	5 pm	"A" Battery. Fired four rounds AX on d.19 & 90.80 in checking registration.	
	22/9	10.30 to 11 am	"D" Battery. 19 rounds fired on d.13 & 6.9; d.13 & 6. and d.19 & 9.8 in registration	
			— do — 12 rounds fired on d.9 a 53/52 at request of Camden Battery.	
	23/9	9.30 am	"D" Battery. Fired 6 rounds on bottle dump at d.8 & 93/52 to 97/48 at request of Camden Battery Group.	
		6.30/6 to 7.30/pm	"A" Battery fired 23 rounds on d.19 & 90/75 : d.8 a 68/78 and d.19 d. 92/18 in calibration.	

Place	Date	Hour	Summary of Events and Information	Appendices
Englebelmer	24/9/16	1.35 to 2.35pm	"D" Battery fired 12 rounds O.K. on enemy battery at d.30.a.58/48. All Batteries. Tasks allotted by Counter Battery as per programme for "V" day attached carried out.	
	25/9/16		All Batteries. Tasks allotted by Counter Battery as per programme attached for "V" Day, carried out.	
	26/9/16		All Batteries. Tasks allotted by Counter Battery for "W" day as per programme attached for "W" Day carried out.	
		12.30pm	do. Task Concentration carried out	
		3.30pm	Guns discharged by Infantry, and all Batteries from barrage in accordance with Operation Orders attached	

Place	Date	Hour	Summary of Events and Information	references to Appendices
Euphrates	27/6		All Batteries. Tasks allotted by Cawnden Battery Group for "Z" day carried out. (programme attached).	
	28/6		All Batteries - Tasks as per programme attached for "Y" day, allotted by Cawnden Battery Group carried out. A & C Batteries fire on gaps in wire, during night in order to keep same open	
			Owing to the climatic conditions "Z" day operations which should have taken place today, were postponed for two days	
	29/6		All Batteries - Tasks as per programme for ½ day carried out.	

1875 Wt. W593/826 1,000,000 4/15 J.B.C. & A. A.D.S.S./Forms/C. 2118.

Place	Date	Hour	Summary of Events and Information	references to Appendices
Enfilades	30/9/16		All Batteries - Lousy and Tasks allotted by Divisional Battery as per Programme attached for Y.B. day.	6/1
		6.30 a		
		9.30 a	A Second intense bombardment of enemy trenches was carried out by all batteries	

J E Earnshaw Capt R.A./fs
for LIEUTENANT COLONEL V.D. R.F.A.
COMDG 247th. (W.R.) BRIGADE R.F.A.

THIEPVAL — ALBERT

We had known it the before the
war having been here to the [?]
to check the orbs terminals day
annuals like he had examined the
distance an arm i/a. It be a
ride (20 min) on the wind forming
and black of grass across 2nd
line
was entirely covered with [?] line
posts.
ARTHUILLE
ALBERT
AVELUY
Loro km to see MARTINSART (?)
Nous descendu
RODER

SECRET URGENT

"Batteries will not fire unless they receive the code word ROBER.

Batteries will fire on all night tasks at double the usual rate of fire —

0.20 to 0.30
0.30 to 1.00
1.20 to 1.30

No firing during the intervals

Acknowledge by quoting
S/6

JE Earnshaw Capt RA
26/6. 247th WR Bde

Secret.   5/5.

O.C. D/247.

    Concentration will take place on the following villages today 26th instant
ST PIERRE DIVION

Positions 76
        78 ⎫ Super-Heavies 1 round per gun.
        79 ⎬ Other natures 2 rounds per gun
        83 ⎭ at 12 noon and again at 5 pm
        89
        91

The first round should be timed to arrive at the hour stated.

The above times are subject to alteration

26/6/16.   J. Barnston Capt. Adjt.
                                     247 Bde R.F.A.

SECRET URGENT

...ogramme of Counter Battery Work.

Hostile guns will be 'marked'

	24th Heavy Battery	F17 & F33*
	108th — —	F8
26 9088	108th — —	
	119th — —	F24 & R29 d 7856
	W. Riding — —	F19

...our Machine ... came under fire, a short
burst (2 minutes ... ... will be fired on each,
... by ... fire at ... irregular
... long as the shelling continues.

If possible the C.B. Battery machine will
engage Co... Batteries ... or more Active
... Batteries during ... ... the day
... ... both Batteries
(to be knocked out) will be engaged ... of the day
... aeroplane Observation.

Bde No	B.F.C. Co.	...	Ammunition
59	F 20	70 S.A.	about 150 Rounds
51·63	F11, F14, F22	105 S.A.	" 300
62	F 29	Heavy	" 300

Before the commencement of our ... of ...
fire (2 minutes ... ... can be ... ...
... ... fire each 18 pr. ... ... will be ...
... the length of similar burst of fire will be fired
... ... fire the commencing of our fire ... ...
... ... the burst will be notified by R.O. Off.
... by ... hours notice being given to the ...
... have received the ... ...
... under ... ...

V

West Riding Brigade

Counter Battery tasks for 'W'

(As for 'V' day)

The following hostile batteries will be engaged during the day with aeroplane observation

RED No	RFC CALL	BATTERY	APPROX AMMN
—	F 33	20 S.G.	150
60	F 23	20 S.B.	150
40	F 16	70 S.B.	
49	F 7	71 S.B.	
51	F 11		
48	F 6	108 S.B.	200

Continuous

And will be ~~maintained~~ be as follows:— at the rates laid down until 'Y' day, unless amended, commencing at once

A/247	8	Rounds	an	hour	on	50
						44
C/247	8	"	"	"	"	62
B/247	8	"	"	"	"	57 Both ans Soul
D/247	4	"	"	"	"	68
24 H.Bry	4	"	"	"	"	59
	4	"	"	"	"	58
129 "	4	"	"	"	"	62
	4	"	"	"	"	66
W.R. H.B	4	"	"	"	"	47
	4	"	"	"	"	66
108 (N)	4	"	"	"	"	51
(S)	4	"	"	"	"	62

(Same as "V" day)

A.C. Haig

20-6-16 — 9 pm   O.C. Left × Corps R.A.

West Riding
Brigade

_____ for "X" day

Same as for "V" day with addition of
R24c 58/45 to close marker by 24 H.B.

The following Hostile Batteries will
be engaged during the day under
Aeroplane observation.

	R.E.D N°	R.F.C. Call	Battery	APPROX: AMMN.
	60	P 28	70 S.B.	100
R22b 40/38	40	P 33	110	100
	70	P 33		
	67	P 31	D247	200
B. bie hagen 3.8	41	P 15	D/247	150
	43	P 6	D247	100
	08	P 20	108 S.B.	200
	50	P 9	108 S.B.	150
	72	P 35	70 S.B.	100

following
As ordered with additions.

D/247   4 Rounds per gun on   69.
11 B.   2   "   "   "   64.
A+C/247 4   "   "   " (Each) on 49.

as for V day.

Battery Commanders when being
ranged by an Aeroplane will on
receipt of the signal "GO" proceed to
and make those
corrections on the "General Recorder" which
they receive from the observer.

On the conclusion of any shoot
contained in the programme this office
will be at once notified.

A.L. Haig
Major R.A.
O.C. South Batteries
X Corps H.A.

Counter Battery Orders for Y day.

West Ridge Brigade

Same as for X day with the alteration that 24th H.B. will sweep road from R.24.c.50.50. to 58.45.

eries.

The following Hostile Batteries will be engaged during the day with aeroplane observation:-

R.F.C. No.	Battery	Approximate rounds.
36	D/247	200
37	D/247.	200
9	108th S.B.	200
12	108th S.B.	200
35	70th S.B.	100
23	20th S.B.	100
26	20th S.B.	150

…e weather remains unfavourable and observation has to …ut from inside our lines, one aeroplane may put several … to their targets at the same time and if this proceedure …atteries must be prepared for the order to open with …attery salvos.

ire.   As ordered with following addition:-

H.B.   2 rounds per hour on R.22.b.90.88.
.B.   2 rounds per hour on R.22.b.90.88.

   As for X day.

                                    Major R.A.,
        O.C. Counter Batteries, Xth Corps H.A.

COUNTER BATTERY ORDERS for Y (2) DAY.

A.A. Guns. Same as for Y day.

Hostile Batteries. The following hostile batteries will be engaged during the day with aeroplane observation:-

Red No.	R.F.C Call.	Battery	Approximate Number of rounds.
-	F.38	20th Siege.	
-	F.37	"	
67	F.31	108th Siege.	To be detailed later.
58	F.12	"	
48	F. 6	70th Siege.	
41	F.15	D/247.	
-	F.40	"	

Continuous Fire will be as follows: all previous orders re continuous fire are cancelled:-

A/247.	12 rounds per hour on 47, 40 and 49.
	8 rounds per hour on 59.
C/247.	8 rounds per hour on 51(N & S) and 63.
	8 rounds per hour on F.42.
	4 rounds per hour on 62.
D/247.	6 rounds per hour on 68, 69.
	2 rounds per hour on 62.
24th H.B.	6 rounds per hour on 68, 69.
	4 rounds per hour on 70.
	2 rounds per hour on COURCELETTE exits.
108th H.B.RX	4 rounds per hour on 51 and 63.
	2 rounds per hour on F.42.
108th H.B.LX	4 rounds per hour on 47, 40 and 49.
	2 rounds per hour on MIRAUMONT exit.
119th H.B.	4 rounds per hour on F.33.
	2 rounds per hour on F.37.
	2 rounds per hour on MIRAUMONT exit.
122nd H.B.	4 rounds per hour on 70 by night.
152nd H.B.	4 rounds per hour on 59 by night.
WRR.H.B.	4 rounds per hour on 66.
	2 rounds per hour on F.33.
	2 rounds per hour on F.37.
	2 rounds per hour on COURCELETTE exits.

N.F. Targets. As for X day.
The order re the signal 'G.O.' published in Counter Battery orders for X day must be strictly adhered to.

Major R.A.,
O.C. Counter Batteries Heavy Artillery X Corps.

29.6.1916.

D/247.

As you will be doing a gas shell job on 2 day from -65 to +30 your task already sent you for that day will remain in abeyance until +30 when you will take it up at that point i.e at

Task I   R 20 a 8.5
     II   R 13 d 7.8 to R 13 b 9.4.
     III   Point C 11

M H Owen Lt Col

23/6/16

Your night task "sunken road" may include at your discretion any portion of day task I i.e firing right up the brook and the trenches beyond.

Z day

(Except on Y night) Sunken road R20b and R15c — 1 Section ....

Time		one Section		this gun	this gun
-65 to +30	All guns Gas shell.				
+30		R20 a 8.5 along sunken road to R15 a 9.10 and to R9 d 6.0 — Bank R15 f 3.0 to 4.4 — R14 b 8.0 to R9 c 7.4 with rounds up to 1.10 between points C9 to C10.		+30 R15d3.5 to R15d7.4	+30 Points C4 to C10
1.15	Lift to R15c 0.5 (Beyond green line)				
2.0	All 4 guns			cease	cease
2.35	Barrage Grandcourt v valley / Ancre Valley R15 b5 & c5 (Rate of fire 1 round per gun per 4 minutes)				
3.30	Stop firing				

Position   Battery
   84.   C/247.

    By day.   Counter Battery.

    By night.   Railway and River Bridges R 7 d 0.2 to
                  R 8 d 2.8.   Wire R 19 b 6.4 to point
                  C 11 and the Valley R 14 b and d (omitting
                  sunken road).

Barrage for
YELLOW Line.   Area R 22.   *Rate of fire 1rd per gun per 2 minute*

      3.10   *Stop firing*

| Zero to plus 30 plus 2 | C/247 D/265 or D/164 (1 Sect.) | 120 60 | "A" "D" | } Whole |

Batteries will search and sweep the areas allotted to them.

After ZERO, fire will be continued by the 4.5" Counter
Battery and one section 32nd Division Artillery at a rate
of one round per gun per minute on all the areas until plus
30 minutes from Zero, but times and rates of fire are liable
to alterations, due to the direction of wind, state of
atmosphere and the tactical situation.

Attention is drawn to instructions regarding the use of
lachrymatory shells filled with S.K.", and subordinate
commanders will be warned that if a sudden change of wind
occurs they are to ask if any modification of the programme is
considered necessary.

On no account will these shells be fired WEST of the enemy's
second line.

Position.   Battery.
   80   A/247.

By day.   Counter Battery.

By Night.   C.T's R 20 d 7.1 to 21 b 9.0 and to
            28 b 6.8 and area (omitting strong
            point in R 21 d) and cross roads
            R 22 a. c and area and light railway
            27 a and 21 d.

            1 Section - Counter Battery.

Barrage for
YELLOW Line. Area R 16. *rate of fire 1 rd per gun per 2 minutes*

3-10.   *Stop firing*

Zero to ~~plus 30~~ plus 2	D/247	120	"A"	Whole
	D/265 or D/164 (1 Sect.)	60	"D"	

Batteries will search and sweep the areas allotted to them.

After ZERO, fire will be continued by the 4.5" Counter Battery and one section 32nd Division Artillery at a rate of one round per gun per minute on all the areas until plus 30 minutes from Zero, but times and rates of fire are liable to alterations, due to the direction of wind, state of atmosphere and the tactical situation.

Attention is drawn to instructions regarding the use of lachrymatory shells filled with S.K.", and subordinate commanders will be warned that if a sudden change of wind occurs they are to ask if any modification of the programme is considered necessary.

On no account will these shells be fired WEST of the enemy's second line.

APPENDIX D.

AREAS TO BE ENGAGED WITH GAS SHELL.

1. Parallelogram contained by R 9 d 40.50.   R 9 d 80.40
   R 15 c 90/50   R 15 d 30/40.

2. Area 100 yards EAST and WEST of Line R 22 c 20/00 to
   R 28 a 30/50.

3. Area 100 yards EAST and WEST of line R 16 b 95/30 to
   R 17 a 00.00.

4. Crescent through R 28 d 00.60 - R 28 c 90.00 - R 34 a 30/40 -
   Depth of area 100 yards each side of centre line.

Time Table.

Time.	Battery.	Rounds.	Target.
-65 to -35	D/245	200	Northern third of "A" *half*
	D/246	200	Centre third of "A"
	D/247	200	Southern third of "A"
	D/164	200	"B"
-30 to Zero.	D/245	150	"C" *half*
	D/246	150	Northern third of "D"
	D/247	150	Centre third of "D"
	D/164	150	Southern third of "D"
Zero to plus 30. *plus 2*	D/247	120	"A" } *Whole*
	D/265 or D/164 (1 Sect.)	60	"D".

Batteries will search and sweep the areas allotted to them.

After ZERO, fire will be continued by the 4.5" Counter Battery and one section 32nd Division Artillery at a rate of one round per gun per minute on all the areas until plus 30 minutes from Zero, but times and rates of fire are liable to alterations, due to the direction of wind, state of atmosphere and the tactical situation.

Attention is drawn to instructions regarding the use of lachrymatory shells filled with S.K.", and subordinate commanders will be warned that if a sudden change of wind occurs they are to ask if any modification of the programme is considered necessary.

On no account will these shells be fired WEST of the enemy's second line.

www.ingramcontent.com/pod-product-compliance
Lightning Source LLC
Chambersburg PA
CBHW080850230426
43662CB00013B/2068